ORCHARD

Also by Benedict Macdonald

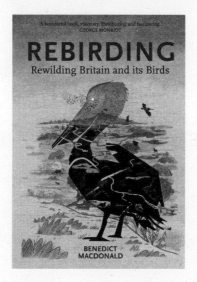

'A splendid new book . . . All rational argument seems to
be on his side'
Guardian

'A wonderful book, visionary, illuminating and fascinating'
George Monbiot

'A wonderfully imaginative book, which shows how things
could be with our rapidly declining areas of countryside,
instead of how – despairingly – they are now'
Rod Liddle

'Visionary yet practical'
New Statesman

'Ben Macdonald has an impressive track record as a field
naturalist, wildlife film-maker and writer, and this passionate,
authoritative, up-to-date and, ultimately, optimistic book is a
worthy comparison to such seminal works as George
Monbiot's *Feral* and Mark Cocker's *Our Place*'
BBC Wildlife

ORCHARD

A YEAR IN ENGLAND'S EDEN

BENEDICT MACDONALD
AND
NICHOLAS GATES

WILLIAM COLLINS

William Collins
An imprint of HarperCollins*Publishers*
1 London Bridge Street
London SE1 9GF

WilliamCollinsBooks.com

First published in Great Britain by William Collins in 2020

Map on pages viii and ix illustrated by Sophie E Tallis
Copyright © Sophie E Tallis 2020
Illustrations on pages 43 and 95 © Alamy Stock Photo
All other illustrations © Shutterstock
Extract from *Ariel* by Sylvia Plath on page 211 reproduced with
permission from the publisher, Faber and Faber Ltd

2021 2023 2022 2020
2 4 6 8 10 9 7 5 3 1

Copyright © Benedict Macdonald and Nicholas Gates, 2020

Benedict Macdonald and Nicholas Gates assert the moral right
to be identified as the authors of this work in accordance with
the Copyright, Designs and Patents Act 1988

A catalogue record for this book is available from the British Library

ISBN 978-0-00-833373-7

Typeset in Berling LT by Palimpsest Book Production Ltd, Falkirk, Stirlingshire
Printed and bound in Great Britain by CPI Group (UK) Ltd, Croydon

DEDICATION

For my parents, Ian and Liz Macdonald. The first of whom patiently helped make over a hundred bird boxes for the orchard. The second of whom patiently read through a hundred drafts of the book.

BENEDICT

For my family, who entertained decades of wild treasures – in various states of decay – being squirrelled around the home, freezer and garden with extreme patience and enduring enthusiasm.

NICHOLAS

Most importantly, for Nancy and David. Wildlife farmers extraordinaire, whose vision and horticulture created *this* orchard Eden long before we were fortunate enough to write about it.

Note: to protect the location of this extraordinary ancient orchard, some names and landmarks in this book have been changed.

CONTENTS

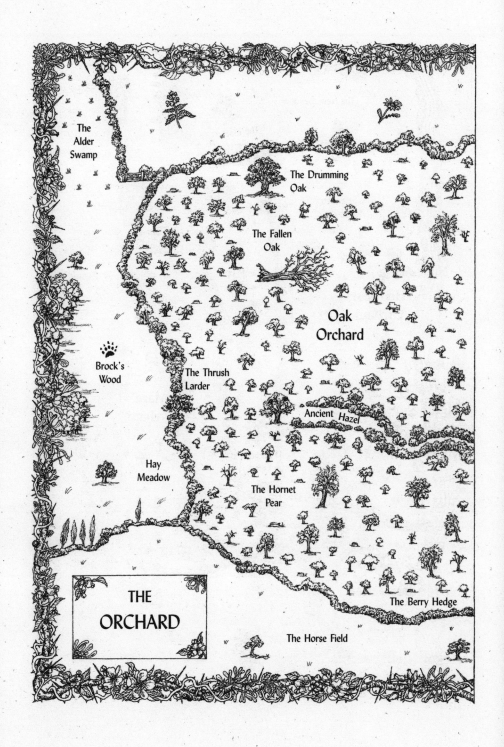

The Alder Swamp

The Drumming Oak

The Fallen Oak

Oak Orchard

Brock's Wood

The Thrush Larder

Ancient Hazel

Hay Meadow

The Hornet Pear

The Berry Hedge

The Horse Field

THE ORCHARD

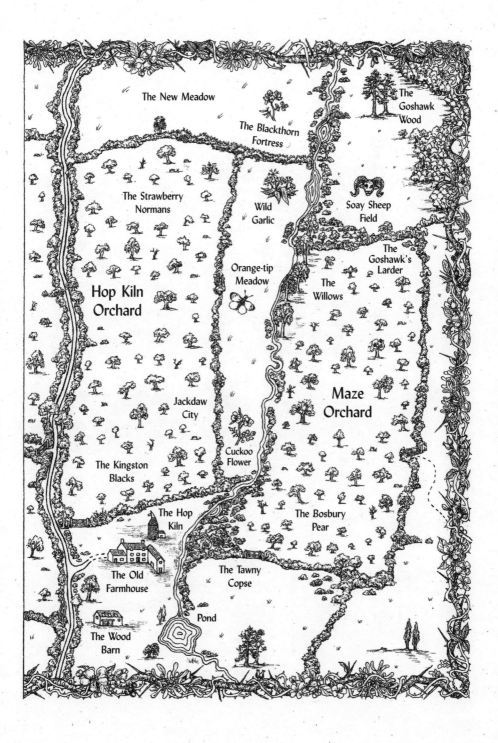

INTRODUCTION

Fiery mist shrouded the drooping furrowed trees. Woodpecker gunfire startled my coffee-primed senses. The song thrush chorus sang so loud, it soon became the jumbled chaos of a dozen raptures. The static fizz of a feeding starling gang carried from the fog-wrapped orchard floor. Well before the sun would rise, Eden was alive.

In a world increasingly starved of life, such moments are special. They burn into our senses. And there are some refuges so cherished, some places so important, some corners of our island so unique, that their wonders *must* be shared. The orchard is one of those places.

Haunted by creatures that may soon become memories – hedgehogs and cuckoos; dormice and bats – this orchard's diversity eclipses that of most nature reserves or designated wild places. It protects, within its boughs, an ark of animals now almost impossible to find living side by side elsewhere in our dying countryside. Yet, like many of nature's best-kept secrets, the orchard's discovery came to me as a surprise.

The visit had begun with another painfully early start: pouring water on my own reproachful face, at five o'clock in the morning, in suburban Bristol; falling into my clothes, and car, then driving north to Herefordshire – the steam of coffee rising. With the sun yet to sail, I nudged my unwilling car into a disused farm gate, bound by twine and locked by ivy. And then – I peered beyond.

Beyond my remit to explore, the mournful sigh of a bullfinch sounded from the nearby hedgerow. Then came the chatter of a redstart. What? You're not supposed to find redstarts here! *'Cuck-oo.'* This, too, was the first time I'd ever heard this sound in an orchard. Then, the drumming of one, two, three lesser spotted woodpeckers! A sound of the older countryside, this chorus brought me to my senses. It was as if every vanishing song in England had been broadcast all at once. What started as a routine survey had transformed into a journey back in time.

Looking at my watch, it was still only six-thirty in the morning. Sharing my enthusiasm for this newfound refuge with its unknown owners this early in the day might not endear them to my quest to discover its secrets. Instead I opened my beaten green thermos and perched quietly on a gatepost.

The mist fermented as the amber sun burned the ridge-line of the Malverns. Finally, Eden's curtain was lifted. This was, most certainly, an orchard. But in place of serried, planted ranks, chopped limbs and neat grass, lay a jumbled, magical chaos. Cutting the orchard in two, a hedgerow of two centuries ago had matured into a line of serpentine oaks. Enormous dead trunks stood where previous apples had perished; encrusted with bracket fungi and cocooned in nettles. The oldest trees were riven with the concentric homes of woodpeckers. The hedgerows were so thick, the sun shunned them: you could scarcely have driven a tank through their midst. This was an orchard gone wild.

Enraptured, I wandered along the lane, seeking the owner of Eden. As the lane turned a corner, the twin peaks of a hop kiln, a building designed for drying hops for brewing, towered into view. A raucous colony of jackdaws erupted from its summit. Before me lay the kind of garden you see in photographs from before the Second World War, or the kind of farm you discover in the rambling countryside of Europe's oldest corners.

Whatever the purpose of the buildings, nature was firmly in control. The walls were thick with hungry, climbing creepers and rife with brambles. The flowerbeds began to drone with bees as the warmth of the sun broke over the garden. The first small tortoiseshells of the morning fluttered past, as they had done in my childhood.

As I reached a neatly painted door, suggesting that a human might also be at home here, I was startled. Right next to the door, surrounded by a duvet of down, a female mallard was sitting on her nest. Her demeanour made it very clear that she lived here as well. I edged nervously around her – then, double-checking that it really was an acceptable hour, I knocked.

English country landowners can be a distinctive and sometimes eccentric bunch. Some carry a strong dislike of anyone walking on their land, as if you might be trampling on their soul. Others simply ignore you, as you might pass by a sheep, nibbling quietly in a field. When a bright-eyed lady let me in, I wasn't sure what to expect. After thanking Nancy for her time, I explained how I'd been surveying orchards for weeks – but as yet, found nothing like hers. I shared quite how many birds were singing in the dawn chorus, and how some of the special ones, such as the lesser spotted woodpecker or the cuckoo were, elsewhere, in critical decline. But as Nancy gently brushed the Mogster – a rug-like Norwegian Forest cat – from its favoured perch beside the stove, her quiet knowing smile made one thing very clear. Nothing I was saying came as a surprise.

Nancy and her son, David, knew exactly how special their orchard was – for the creatures whom they permitted to run it. The enormous dead stumps, beloved by woodpeckers, were left not through neglect but by design. The spiky piles of brash were left for hedgehogs: the surplus fallen fruit, to help thrushes through the winter. A fruit farmer, a cider-maker, Nancy most certainly was – as her family had been for generations. But the more I listened and learned, the more I realised Nancy was perhaps the best wildlife farmer that I'd ever met.

Nancy knew not only which trees the woodpeckers drummed in, but in which pile of fallen branches the local hedgehog spent his time. She kept the hedgerows thick and high on purpose, knew which part of her attic held lesser horseshoe bats, and where, in a few months' time, the spotted flycatchers would nest in her wisteria. Nancy knew that no chemical had touched her land since 1930, and, believed that this might account for the extraordinary abundance of declining species in her orchard. Before we knew it, we had both worked our way through a pot of tea.

It had been an inspirational meeting, and now, cautiously, I ventured the question I'd been burning to ask. Might *I* be let loose into Eden? There was a pregnant silence – and then, Nancy agreed. After promising to feed back every natural secret of the land she owned – a promise we have kept to this day – I was set free. Like a giddy schoolboy, or Tigger, I bounded through the gate marked 'no public right of way' – and out into the orchard. Three years later, I would still be bounding around.

In 2014, I drove east to Suffolk, to work on the BBC series *Springwatch*. James, my producer, phoned me to explain that he'd paired me with 'someone as fanatical about nature as yourself'. On arrival at our lodgings, I met Nick. In my car boot, I had a collection of old birds' nests from the orchard. Nick was unloading a fine pair of antlers, which he'd collected in Ashdown Forest. We'd spend the next three weeks monitoring the wildlife cameras of the popular BBC series. Working night shifts, we'd wait on the edge of our seats for the badgers to come out. In this time, we traded all the stories of two people who'd been raising insects, and watching wildlife, since the time we could first read.

By early 2015, Nick, now a good friend, moved to Bristol to build his own career as a wildlife film-maker. Immediately, he asked where we would adopt as our new local patch. By now, Eden held me in its spell: 'you have to see this place', I told him.

For the next five years, we would drive most weekends through the empty, chemical fields and flailed hedgerows that constitute the countryside handed down to our generation. We would pass the ghostly apple trees of one-time orchards around Gloucester, and drive through farmlands so silent that absurd, confused pheasants were the commonest of birds. But we knew that when we arrived in Eden, everything would change. Nature was about to turn up the volume. We were determined to record her every note.

Soon, hundreds of pages of field notes, nest records and diagrams were pouring in. We realised that our one adopted orchard was in fact split into three distinct sections, all neighbours, similar on first impression but each holding their own personality and charm. Between us, we would slowly learn 'The Orchard Rules'. How it worked. What drove its diversity. Who lived here, died here – and *why*.

Each year, we have witnessed, marvelled and been continually amazed at the true exuberance of our orchard's wildlife. The wild bounty of a traditional orchard, we decided, is too special to be handed down in poems or written histories alone.

We will not be the last generation to hear the orchard sing. Orchards should, and must, live on. And so, we decided to share the wonders of this fading paradise with you. We want you, like us, to understand its inhabitants, to share their journeys, to live and laugh among the creatures of the orchard.

Told across twelve months, we want to share with you the richness of England's Eden – as the changing seasons bring surprise, success and struggle. We want to unveil the beauty of our last, traditional orchards – through the wary eyes, and watchful ears, of just *one*.

But before we do so, it's time to share another journey – and that is the journey of the orchard itself. So first, we need to travel far to the east, to a distant land and a forgotten time – where the English orchard's remarkable story begins with a very hungry bear.

APPLES and BEARS

A BRIEF HISTORY OF
THE ENGLISH ORCHARD

This orchard's story does not begin with bucolic, cider-making monks in a Medieval monastery. Nor does it begin with enterprising Romans, grafting and planting apples in the Mediterranean. The story is far older, far wilder – and infinitely more unlikely – and it begins not with an apple but a bear.[1]

This orchard's story begins in the world's largest land-locked country: a country most of us will never visit, yet whose very name conjures a blank, mysterious canvas in our minds. Here in the Tian Shan mountains of Kazakhstan, lies a world so remote from the hills of our own island that its highest rocks are still scratched by the padded claws of snow leopards. Each autumn here, below the glare of piercing blue air and white ice peaks, a bushy, haphazard forest glows red as the seasons change. Strewn across the high montane slopes, there is something both familiar and strange about these woodlands to the European eye. The vivid colours of the trees, glowing in the mountain light, are more like those of Canadian maples. But these wide, bushy trees also have mistletoe on them. And hanging in their boughs, redder than any of the turning leaves, glow red, juicy apples.

Here lies original Eden. The apple trees growing on these slopes are those of *Malus sieversii*. This is the wild apple endemic to central Asia and beloved by the local people of the Almaty region, formerly known as Alma-ata, which translates as the 'father of apples'. These are among the world's only and last wild apple forests. Ancient trees, intertangled and intertwined, do not grow in the neat lines of England's more orderly orchards, but cover the mountainside in rambling groves. Carpets of golden windfalls range in size from marbles to cricket balls.[2] By all accounts, their tastes vary even more. On one tree, the fruit may grow sweet and plummy: on the next, acerbic and bitter. Yet over millennia, the size and grandeur of these fruits has been altered and selected. And this is where the bear comes in.

These idyllic slopes, rich not only in apples but in berries, hips and haws, are a foraging paradise for a gardener long lost to British woodlands. Into these wild groves each autumn come dozens of brown bears. The mountain winter is approaching, and soon they must be tucked up, safe in their hibernation caves. First, bears must pile on the calories to see them through the freezing dark – and the Tian Shan apples provide them with just that. In spite of their urge to eat, bears are fussy foragers. Like us, they have a sweet tooth. Bitter apples do not appeal to a bear's palate, and so, for many generations, they have chosen only the sweetest apples from this rambling lottery of fruit. The seeds of these juicy, sweet apples pass through the bear's gut intact. Recent visitors to these mountains have found bear droppings burgeoning with apple seeds.[3] And the following spring, from each bear toilet on this mountain, bursts a new, slightly sweeter apple tree. Bears, then, have been cultivating apples far longer than the earliest orchard grower in Europe, selectively breeding the world's apple trees long before they would make an incredible migration – from Kazakhstan to Kent and far beyond.

The actions of bears on the slopes of Tian Shan are a reminder of a question few of us might think to ask today – why do apple trees yield apples at all? Far from ecological goodwill, an apple's fruits are, quite simply, an advertisement to would-be seed dispersers to plant its kindred far and wide. But while flowers can rely on airborne pollinators, and small seeds can be carried by birds, only far larger animals can be relied upon to transport apple pips, intact, over large distances. The latest research suggests that large-fruiting trees, such as our own native crab apples, as well as those apples of the wild Kazakh forests, developed, in the million-year time-frame, to attract the attention not only of large animals, but of giants.

Though horses, bears and boar, of Europe's surviving fauna, are capable of dispersing apple seeds, a number of lost herbivores, such as the Giant Deer, are thought to have played an ever more important role in carrying and planting apple seeds over truly vast distances. Indeed, analysis of the Kazakh apple gene pool has shown that in the last ten thousand years, with many of the far-roaming Eurasian mega-herbivores extinct, wild apples would then have been dispersed far shorter distances than before, by smaller, more sedentary animals such as our bears.[4]

In an ecologically vast timeframe, wild fruit trees would have developed a profound ecological importance for Eurasia's native wildlife, being planted and dispersed by giants. Even today, the high canopy spikes of Europe's native crab apple trees are a striking reminder that straight-tusked elephants would once have posed an enormous nuisance to our fruit trees; browsing far higher than any living animal can reach. Yet at the same time, Eurasia's once abundant elephants would also have planted apple trees across vast swathes of its land mass, by carrying seeds in their dung [5]

THE GREAT MIGRATION

Deep in the caves above the Kazakh apple forests, petro-glyphs etched into the rocks remind us that its fruit glades were an Eden for early humans too. Long before the grafting and the unnatural selection of trees, people, with their fondness for all things sweet, would also have altered these orchards – in much the same way as bears. As cores were tossed away each year, slightly sweeter fruit trees, bearing larger apples, would have grown the season after: unnatural selection at work. But how, from this lofty world, deep in the Kazakh mountains, did the apple tree break free?

The next player in our early orchard drama is, most likely, a horse. Wild horses, now confined largely to Mongolia and referred to by the locals there as *takhi*, or 'spirit horses', once roamed widely across the steppes of Eurasia. But the Kazakhs had also tamed horses very early on. The latest evidence suggests that the Botai culture, of Kazakhstan's Akmola province, was among the first to have the idea of domesticating horses – and were harnessing and milking these as early as 5,500 years ago.[6] If bears and Neanderthal foragers are responsible for the early selection of the world's wild apple stock, horses most likely played a role in transporting that stock from its remote source – abroad. These domestic horses, of course, moved at human behest – and this is where the Silk Road comes in.

The improbable migration of the apple tree would never have happened at all were it not for the fact that the Silk Road came to pass directly through Almaty province. Here, it is believed that as the parched silk traders travelled through, they scrumped like schoolchildren en-route.[7] Travelling westwards, they would have planted apples with accidental abandon, as they tossed apple cores from horseback. Horses too, infamously fond of apples, would have transported embryonic trees in their dung. Over centuries, this protracted pomenary pooing procession would take the apple on an incredible journey. And so, from an obscure endemic of the Kazakh slopes, the world's most iconic fruit tree is thought to have migrated westwards – and into Europe.

Only as recently as 2010 have scientists finally pieced together how a wild tree, confined to the mountains of Kazakhstan, expanded to shape the landscape, culture and literature of the western world. Sequencing the genome of the domestic apple, *Malus domesticus*, scientists unravelled a fiendishly complex network of 57,000 different genes. Tracing these genes back in time, it was found that their origins *all* lay in wild Kazakh apples. The apples we eat and cultivate today have descended almost exclusively from the slopes of Almaty. And virtually every cultivated apple growing in our country, and indeed across most of the world, has come to us from the bear-gardened foothills of one mountain range in Kazakhstan.[8]

Genealogical evidence proves that some trees, planted by now deliberately, would then have cross-pollinated with Europe's native crab-apples. While the Kazakh apple genes make for large, plump apples, the crab apple's genes contribute towards a more robust fruit. The world's most successful hybrid had been born.

By 2000 BCE, the now domesticated apple had reached the eastern Mediterranean. Apples then headed west – and they arrived in time to feature in Homer's *Odyssey*, written in the eighth or ninth century BCE. Literature's first mention of a deliberately-planted orchard can be found when Odysseus visits the court of King Alcinous; admiring, on his arrival, an enticing walled grove of 'beautiful trees – pears, pomegranates, and the most delicious apples'.[9]

Apples in literature would soon become irresistible. In one Greek myth, one unusually disruptive apple is chucked into a crowded party by Eris, the goddess of strife and discord, labelled simply 'to the fairest'. Not renowned for their modesty, the guests Hera, Aphrodite and Athena all think the apple is addressed to them. Jealous fights erupt and all hell breaks loose.[10] In another, stranger story, the nimble Atalanta seeks to escape a boring life of marriage by running faster than any of her prospective husbands and beating them in a race. Hippomenes, however, has been entrusted with three golden apples by Aphrodite, and carefully lays these ahead of Atalanta. She slows down, picking them up to eat them, and this allows Hippomenes to catch her up – thereby winning her hand in marriage.[11]

By 300 BCE, writers like Virgil and Cato were already naming not one, but dozens of breeds of apple. Pliny was describing how fruiterers would auction the fruit on their trees.[12] The Romans had been busy, and were now grafting and adapting apples to their different climates. The custom of naming breeds after important people, or places, such as the Armerian and Cestine, began. As the Roman armies marched north into France, the apple would follow. But even if the Romans had the skills to craft wonderful apple groves in Rome, there is little evidence that theirs were the hands to firmly establish Britain's first homegrown orchards.

SAXONS, MONKS AND QUEENS

'Orchard' originates from the Old English word, *ortgeard*. The first part of this word draws on the Latin *hortus*, meaning garden. The second part is the Old English word for yard. By the late era of Old English, the word had evolved from 'garden yard' to mean 'fruit garden'.[13] And given orchards evolved so early in our history that our very language was evolving alongside them, tracing how orchards were first cultivated in Britain has greatly challenged historians.

As long ago as 854 CE, the Vale of Taunton's Orchard Portman village was named 'Orceard', though this most likely referred to a general fruit-growing area.[14] The Anglo-Saxon food-rent lists, however, show little awareness or description of anything recognisable as an apple; '*æppel*', in Old English, referred to a range of different fruits.[15]

Just after the arrival of the Normans, the Domesday Book records just one extensive apple orchard in England.[16] But now, the Normans, already familiar with the successful cultivation of apples in their own country, having inherited that in turn from fruit-growers in the Mediterranean region, would kick-start orchards as we know them today. By the late tenth century, manuscript plans of the Christ Church monastery in Canterbury show a 'pomeranium', or apple garden, consisting of apples and pears.[17] *Pearmain*, a variety of cultivated dessert apple first recorded in 1204, is the oldest cultivated apple name recorded in English.[18] By the twelfth century, Wardoun pears were being cultivated in England, at Bedfordshire's Warden Abbey.[19]

According to orchard historian Jim Chapman, the marriage of Henry III to Eleanor of Provence led to a 'renaissance' in the English orchard, as the scions of culinary Cailhou pears were planted in royal gardens. Some, Jim argues, like those seeded in the Queen's garden at Everswell, were radiant with blossom; perhaps more suited to ornament than the practical growing of fruit. It was in part from the royal court that monks such as those of Llanthony Priory received and cultivated further breeds.[20] By 1275, Battle Abbey was also selling cider to the public, and, by 1333, the poems of cleric William of Shoreham record the first known appearance of the word syder in the English language'.[21] Until their dissolution, the monasteries would continue to propagate orchards and spread them around Britain.

By the fourteenth century, the climate was changing. In a prolonged period of cooler, wetter weather, vineyards in England became increasingly unproductive for the monks, who had pioneered viticulture in many areas such as Gloucestershire during warmer, drier times. As it does today, England fell back on the easier route of importing its best wine from overseas. We began to grow apples, and orchards, in place of vines. Across the fourteenth century, orchards would continue to expand across our country.

But after the ravages of the Black Death, multiple outbreaks of the plague and the War of the Roses, apple cultivation somewhat slipped down the list of national priorities in the late fourteen and fifteen hundreds. As late as 1585, Richard Drake, a curate from the Malverns, commented that Black Worcester cultivated pears provided such poor harvest that local people were reduced to foraging wild crab apples to make perry instead.[22] The orchard's story only picks up again with Henry VIII – and his 'fruiterer', Richard Harris.

THE ORCHARD EMPIRE

Henry VIII was notoriously fond of his food. In addition to the bitterns, woodcocks and wild boar that piled his plates, Henry had a sweet tooth, too. He was fond of fruits and artichokes, while Anne Boleyn was particularly partial to cherries.[23]

Henry tasked Richard Harris with no mean challenge; to scour the western world for its best fruit varieties, bring them back to England – and grow them. Close to Teynham in Kent lie the long-established fruit-growing regions known to some as 'The Garden of England'. Here, Richard established what became known as the King's Orchards. These were 'mother' orchards that would serve as the nation's repository of world-class apple stock. Richard, it seemed, was incredibly competent. His peer, William Lambarde, noted how Richard had visited the Low Countries, bringing from there 'cherrie grafts and Pear grafts of diverse sorts'. Lambarde also noted that 'our honest patriote Richard Harrys planted by his great coste and rare industrie, the sweet Cherrie, the temperate pipyn, and the golden Renate'.[24] England had caught up with the Greeks and the Romans. Now, we too were rewriting Eden and creating new fruits.

From these Teynham orchards, new breeds made their way out across the country. Kent became the first county to receive and grow the 'pippin'. This word, which sounds quintessentially English, is – we were a little sad to discover – French. Pippin means 'seedling'. These seedlings were brought by Harris from France.[25]

Across the sixteenth and especially the seventeenth century, the overall low point for woodland cover in

Britain's history, it does seem possible that our fastest-expanding forests were orchards, as fruit-growing areas spread out from the capital of Kent. Lambarde observed that Teynham, 'with thirty other parishes lying on each side of this porte way, and extending from Raynham to Blean Wood, be the Cherrie gardein, and Apple orcharde of Kent'.[26] Few traces can be found on modern aerial maps of this fruit forest, which would once have been greater in scale than many natural woodlands at this time. Soon, the landscapes and economies of whole counties would become shaped by the orchard. During England's brief Commonwealth, lasting from 1649 to 1660, Oliver Cromwell decreed a national initiative to plant fruit trees across the country. While this never came to full fruition, many further orchards were planted in Herefordshire, Gloucestershire and Worcestershire.[27]

It seems extraordinary now to Nick and me, driving through Herefordshire to our adopted ancient orchard, an island of wood pasture forest in a lifeless sea of crops, that the whole of Herefordshire was once, in the words of John Evelyn, writing in 1664, 'one entire orchard'.[28] John Beale, writing about the county in 1657, observed that 'from the greatest persons to the poorest cottager, all habitations are encompassed with orchards and gardens; and in most places our hedges are enriched with rows of fruit trees'.[29] Herefordshire must have been quite an extraordinary place to take a horse and cart through in the seventeenth century. To see nothing but fruit forests, especially when in flower, must have been an unforgettable spectacle.

While most natural historians now recognise Herefordshire and Worcestershire as the vital last strongholds of our ancient orchards, we have forgotten that huge apple forests grew across the south-west, too, so completely have these vanished from the landscape. By the seventeenth century, Somerset was an orchard powerhouse. One hundred and fifty-six apple varieties are associated with its largely lost orchards – and the scale of these was remarkable. As late as the turn of the nineteenth century, 21,000 acres of Somerset lay under apples. Devon, at the same time, had up to 23,000 acres in all.

Cider-making, rather than the sale of apples, powered the growth of these orchard counties. By the onset of the industrial revolution, many of Britain's older forms of farmland, such as the hay meadow, were set to vanish as agriculture started to intensify. Orchards, remaining commercially viable, adapted far better to the advent of industrial farming. New canals meant an expansion in the market for cider. By 1800, it was estimated that ten thousand hogsheads – equating to roughly five million litres of cider – were being shipped out of Worcestershire alone on an annual basis. By 1877, between the counties of Somerset, Devon, Herefordshire, Worcestershire, Gloucestershire and Kent, there were 89,000 acres of orchards.[30] Many of these had been maturing for centuries. In doing so, these new agricultural habitats would recreate something very old and special for our native wildlife.

APPLES AND BEARS

THE NEW WILD WOOD

While forests of wild fruit trees have not been seen in most of Britain for a very long time, fossil evidence suggests that they once played a vital role in Britain's ecological history. Aurochs (wild cattle which stood over two metres tall), wild horses, boar, elk (moose), red and roe deer would all have been shifted around the landscape by the predation pressures of brown bears, wolves and lynx. Bears, boar and horses, in particular, would have vectored the seeds of fruit trees in their dung as they moved around the landscape, planting new 'orchards' across the wood pastures of Britain.

Salisbury Plain is now thought to have been a landscape once dotted with vast, roaming herds of wild herbivores, such as aurochs, horses and deer. The beetle and snail fossil record suggests that this tree-studded grassland, Britain's Serengeti, would have been dominated not by dense groves of shady trees – but by open groves of wild apples, cherries, hawthorns and sloes.[31] The name Avalon is believed to mean 'the isle of apples', a name given to Glastonbury's distinctive hill in the Iron Age, when native crab-apples would have studded its steep slopes.[32]

These days, the ramshackle beauty of wild English fruit groves is now a rare sight indeed. But in the oldest pasture woods of the New Forest you can still find crab apples growing in wild formation. Here, free-roaming ponies and their foals graze gently around wild-sown fruit trees, much as their ancestral tarpan would have done eight thousand years before.

By the seventeenth century, Britain had been comprehensively deforested not over centuries but millennia – and this period marked the overall low point of woodland cover on our island. Yet with the wild wood long gone, maturing orchards – spacious wood pastures rich in vital processes of decay – would echo a lost habitat that British wildlife inherently understands. Our forgotten wood pastures, and their free-roaming wild herbivores, were given a strange reincarnation in the orchard.

Whole animal orders which had developed in old-growth wood pastures – from wood-decay beetles to woodpeckers and bats – would have found orchards a new home, and moved into them as they matured. Orchards became a unique fusion of agricultural and primeval woodland – an anachronistic refuge, surviving for centuries after the original wild wood had gone.

In addition to an orchard's ability to mimic ancient wild habitats, if left in traditional and unfettered form, orchards act as havens of insect life. *Malus* apple trees have evolved enormous insect diversity over time. At least ninety-three species specialise in living in their branches. When the eminent botanist Thomas Southwood analysed the insect life of Britain's trees, his study found that much of the apple's richness lay in its ability to harbour tiny lives – particularly beetles, micromoths, true bugs and flowerbugs – which then build a food-chain upwards from the bottom.

Plants and lichens, many specialising in mature fruit trees, such as the orchard's tooth fungus, harbour herbivorous insects. These in turn are followed by armies of small omnivores or predators: wasps, hornets, hoverflies and spiders – and *their* predators in turn. Huge reserves of saproxylic species, those specialising in dead wood, feast around old fruit trees. Delving deeper, you discover food-chains within food-chains. Mistletoe, for example, harbours the mistletoe marble moth, a specialist weevil and four other insects unique to its tenacious tangle of vegetation.

Perhaps the greatest reminder that Britain's wildlife is intrinsically adapted to a life around ancient fruit trees is the noble chafer beetle. Now one of Britain's rarest beetles, confined largely to traditional orchards and the ancient wood pastures of the New Forest, its larval stage occurs only within the decaying trunks of the oldest open-grown fruit trees. A whole range of other species, such as the now lost black-veined white butterfly, whose caterpillars feed on fruit trees, or the wryneck, thriving best in the lightly-grazed anthills between old orchard standards, remind us that our native ecology evolved around wild fruit trees long before people planted them here by design.

As so many wildwood species moved into orchards and flourished, our traditional orchards have become increasingly important havens, prolonging the lives of thousands of creatures that once thrived in our wooded island, millennia ago.

EDEN'S FALL

Few forms of agriculture, so beneficial to wildlife, have had such a short lifespan in our history as the orchard. Still expanding in the 1600s, less than three hundred years later orchards would begin to vanish once more. As early as the late eighteenth century, Devon and Herefordshire cider manufacture fell into decline. Canker decimated many of the trees here, but more damaging was the revelation that the contemporary method of cider manufacture was causing lead poisoning. Sales plummeted. In 1837, tariffs placed on imported fruit, which had encouraged the planting of new orchards, especially in Kent, were dropped – and the apple market collapsed. Kentish cooking apples were turned into cider, which proved of such poor quality that it led to protests.[33]

Soon, the madness of importing from overseas what we, as a country, grow best, would begin. Towards the end of the nineteenth century, two keen orchard lovers in Herefordshire, a Dr Hogg and Dr Bull, lamented how the power of steam – now fuelling trade across the sea and land alike – 'lessens expenditure by cheapness of conveyance'. They note how 'competition becomes world-wide . . . to individuals and localities the result is often ruinous'.[34] Hogg and Bull were well aware that centuries of crafting and changing apples to suit every taste and variety, and of producing a suite of fruits more varied than any we see in our supermarkets today, were coming to an end. And so they wrote an extraordinary book.

Published in 1878, the *Herefordshire Pomona* preserved, forever, an illustrated record of the astonishing 432 varieties of apple and pear that had, over centuries, been cultivated within the county. The lurid 3-D apples drawn by its illustrators, Alice Blanche Ellis and Edith Elizabeth Bull, still leap from the page over a century later, as if waiting keenly to be eaten. From the Sheep's Snout to the Tom Putt, the Eggleton Styre to the Hagloe Crab, the Bastard Rough Coat to the Bloody Turk, the immensely rich culinary heritage of our orchards shines in reds, greens and yellows from every page. Yet when it comes to the wildlife that once lived in these planted wildwoods, we have often come to realise its importance long after these habitats were taken away.

Northamptonshire's Lord Lilford, a keen naturalist, gives us some insight into the richness of his orchards around Badby, in Northamptonshire. He writes of the lesser spotted woodpecker that it is 'certainly now the most common of our three species of woodpecker in this neighbourhood, and we have observed it in every part of the county with which we have any acquaintance'. Of the spotted flycatcher, he notes that 'this little summer visitor is so common and so well known in our county that a very few words will suffice with regard to it'.[35]

Comparing our Malvern orchard notes to those of two centuries ago, Nick and I are struck by certain recurring stories. One of the great forefathers of modern naturalists, Gilbert White, observes of mistle thrushes that 'the people of Hampshire and Sussex call the missel-bird the storm-cock, because it sings early in the spring in blowing showery weather; its song often commences with the year: with us it builds much in orchards'. Our notes show mistle thrushes singing by late December, and placing their first nests in mistletoe as early as February. White also describes redstarts as we have come to know them, not as birds of pure deciduous woodland, but those benefiting from the fruit-growing landscape. 'Sitting very placidly on the top of a tree in a village, the cock sings from morning to night . . . and loves to build in orchards and about houses; with us he perches on the vane of a tall maypole.' [36] One of our adopted orchard's redstarts sings often from a hop kiln – and shows little fear of people. That there are still little windows of connection between White's orchard and ours is quite consoling.

Some of the best natural histories of lost orchards come from the observations of Kentish naturalists, compiled in R.J. Balston's *Notes on the Birds of Kent*, published in 1907. Balston describes the orchard landscape of the Kentish hills: 'on its sides grow the best of hops and the best of orchards . . . It seems that birds of all descriptions could find a home to their liking upon it.'[37]

Many observations concern 'snake birds', which were, at this time, common across Kent's orchards, and had been, until the mid-nineteenth century, a charismatic bird of England's wood-pasture-dominated counties:

> The well-known 'Snake-Bird' after its arrival becomes sparingly distributed over the county, and is generally found in the old woods and orchards, which are well stocked with old gnarled stumps and half-decayed trees, in which the bird can find holes and large cavities for a nesting place.

Known to us as the wryneck, many Kentish naturalists adopted the term 'snake bird' in their writings. Wrynecks, dependent on large volumes of anthills, and thus the lightest of grazing regimes by cattle, were a species that once called commonly across English orchards. Mr W.H. Power, the attentive author of 'The Birds of Bainham', written in 1865, observed that 'in general [the wryneck] is to be heard all over the orchards, and I have several times, by means of a call, brought three at once into a tree within a yard of my head, where they would remain for some time, staring about in the most ludicrous manner'. [38] Today, the wryneck is vanished entirely from our country; traditional orchards one of its last strongholds in Kent – before they were grubbed away.

If wrynecks fascinated those wandering Kent's orchards in the 1800s, other birds were considered less of a welcome arrival. Into Kent's cherry orchards came finches by the dozen. But only one bird, the grumpy-looking hawfinch, has uniquely adapted to crack cherry kernels, with its enormously powerful secateurs of a bill. 'Hawfinches and bullfinches have become very plentiful, and of late years the latter have become a perfect plague to the fruit growers,' writes Balston. It seems an odd thing to imagine now, with fewer than one thousand hawfinches left in Britain, and virtually none in our orchards, that this most elusive woodland bird was once considered a pest.

Yet even the best-recorded natural history of orchards, that of the birds that once sang in The Garden of Kent, is now just that – history. The traditional, mature cherry, apple and pear orchards that once harboured wrynecks and garden warblers, hordes of marauding finches and probably far greater riches, have vanished from the map. And for all their cultural importance, and the huge areas of our country they once covered, the full *natural* history of orchards was never written at all.

Throughout the twentieth century, their economic output increasingly obsolete in the face of expanding cereal farms and the reduced profitability of smaller farms for cider-making, traditional orchards were grubbed relentlessly from the British countryside. Vast areas of Somerset's orchards vanished in a tiny space of time. To this day, the distribution map shows a virtual absence of lesser spotted woodpeckers across most of its former range in the south-west. This bird, like many others, committed to orchards as a habitat far richer, more productive, than the country-side around. But when orchards vanished, the distribution of entire species shifted and reduced on a massive scale.

Since the 1950s, a further 90 per cent of traditional orchards have been lost. As with the destruction of so many other habitats, the EU's Common Agricultural Policy has hastened the demise of orchards – as it has hastened the demise of the countryside itself. Across the 1970s and '80s in particular, many orchard owners have been paid to grub old orchards, in favour of fast-profit forms of farming.[39] Now, only a few traditional orchard landscapes remain in our country.

LAST OF THE ORCHARDS

While the People's Trust for Endangered Species has iden-tified 35,000 traditional orchards still growing across

England,[40] the extent of these, crucial to the preservation of large wildlife populations, has dramatically withdrawn, leaving many as isolated postage stamps within a sterile wider world. When an ecosystem collapses, the fragments that remain are often too small, or scattered, to save; to remain intelligible to the wildlife that inhabited them. Only in a few tiny pockets of western England do enough traditional orchards remain for them to persist, age and grow back over the coming decades.

In Worcestershire, the Teme Valley, the Severn Vale and the Vale of Evesham retain good concentrations of traditional orchards, but those surrounding and within the Wyre Forest, benefiting from its deciduous diversity, preserve extraordinary riches. In a survey of just three traditional orchards in the Wyre, a comprehensive survey recently unearthed the existence of a staggering 1,868 species of wild plants and animals. This, in turn, was extrapolated from the examination of more than 16,000 living specimens within its confines.[41]

Herefordshire, however, remains, as it has been for centuries, Britain's greatest orchard refuge. Distinct areas of the county act as time-capsules, not only for cider-making but the chaotic assemblage of animal life that once thrived across the county. From the meadowland orchards of Bromyard to the rich cider orchards of Much Marcle, woodpeckers and bats, owls and beetles, all thrive side by side as they once did across the whole county centuries before. But the greatest refuge of all lies elsewhere.

From Ledbury, north to the Wyre Forest, fringing the western shadow of the Malvern Hills, the satellite map clearly reveals one of the largest, most aged and most important deciduous woodlands in our country. Shamefully, it has no clear name – though it most certainly should in future years. Now unprecedented in the fractured English countryside, unbroken willow stands, oak parklands, outgrown hedges, dense deciduous copses and traditional orchards run in fine but continuous lines along the shadow of these hills for eighty kilometres. Here lies the largest concentration of traditional orchards left in Britain. And somewhere herein lies our second home.

Welcome to *Orchard*. It's January. The fruits have fallen – and an army of raucous Vikings are once again rampaging across the English countryside.

JANUARY

A WORLD ON THE MOVE

NICK

Rattling around the Earth's wide pause,
a fieldfare – tentative – adamant
. . . emboldened by snow-stolen fields.

NICOLA HEALEY

An acerbic easterly tries to claw its way inside my gaiters. I'm glad to have opted for ski socks this morning; the seasonal 'Beast from the East' is due to arrive any day. Either side of the exposed footpath lie hundreds of acres of arable farmland – cloaked in a thick hoarfrost. It's an unforgiving landscape. At this time of year, the open ground offers little of value to wildlife seeking food and shelter. There are sometimes roe deer, and even the occasional hare, but even they can't brave such brutal conditions. Eden lies just a quarter of a mile ahead, but you'd be forgiven for not believing that if you were standing here.

The remains of a spider web lie draped in the grass – the fine silk lattice iced into a giant broken snowflake. The frost has fossilised the footprints of recent travellers. Big dog. Little dog. Fox. Pheasant. Ah, badger. A broad pad, resembling scaled-down bear tracks etched into the earth. Five round toes, each tipped with fine claw indents. These are fresh; perhaps even from last night, before the frost came in. The heavy clay soil forms an excellent texture for footprints in the winter. Following the tracks, my mind imagines a badger ambling its way down the path: its gait implies a light trot. This animal was moving with purpose; it knew exactly where it was going. It wasn't even distracted by a fresh molehill; the newly-evicted earthen pyramid now signed by the front right paw of a single-minded badger.

After a couple of hundred metres, it became apparent that Brock had been headed in the same direction as I was. Badgers *love* apples. This one had been putting in three steps for each of my own. Dumpy little legs are excellent for digging but not great for locomotion. In a conflict, badgers rarely opt for flight: this is an animal that digs up wasp nests for fun.

Finally, variety. A hedgerow towers through the white morning air. Long daggers of sloe and hawthorn paint over a vibrant injection of colour. Blood red, the fruit of the dog rose is a welcome addition to the blanched winter palette. Agile redwings, able to navigate the razor-wire defences of these trees, burst away from me as I near the orchard's defensive walls.

Tracking the spiky hedge a few dozen more steps, it veers right. And then, without warning, the entire landscape is transformed. Now buffered by the hedgerow, the easterly wind is drowned out as the soundscape hits. The surrounding farmland is as lifeless as the winter South Pole. Yet our adopted orchard is alive.

The scene is too much to process in one glance. Standing at the corner of this sprawling tangled world, a diverse barrage of noise roars from the leafless trees; an out-of-sync ensemble generated by a spectacle increasingly rare in western Europe: a super-abundance of feeding songbirds. It's like stepping back a century – to the halcyon days of the Victorian naturalists; a scene that Darwin and Wallace would have recognised.

'Tack-tack-tack'. The repeating alarm notes of a song thrush. 'Tzeeee. Tzeeeeeeeee'. A greenfinch announces his presence. A powerful little resonating trill fires out of the thorns as a wren deftly disappears back into the hedgerow. Walking further into the orchard, between aged Kingston Blacks and perry pears, a conveyor belt of movement lies ahead. A sweet aroma, the hybrid of fresh silage and a forgotten fruit basket, betrays an abundance of rotting apples below every tree. Taking aim through binoculars, the mirage ahead turns into living chaos, as dozens of fieldfares rotate between the lower branches and the bounty lying under the trees. The ground around their chosen tree shimmers with grey, as these large dumpy thrushes work energetically to pick apart the winter's windfall. The fieldfares take it in turns – each spending no more than a minute on the ground before resuming watch-duty for the others. The more you look, the more you see. A careful scan of the surrounding trees reveals an extensive feeding flock of at least five hundred fieldfares. This orchard – a postage stamp, relative to the size of the surrounding landscape – is giving them exactly what they need to get through the winter: a seasonal magnet in an empty land.

These Vikings are fleeting visitors. Fieldfares breed in Scandinavia and north-eastern Europe. Yet as little as a month after fledging, the first snow arrives in their home-lands. From September onwards, huge numbers descend on eastern England, drawn by the genetic memory of richer pastures. In a particularly cold Nordic winter, up to a million birds can arrive,[1] favouring the more temperate climate of our ocean-warmed island. Today, the mercury registers a brisk one degree Celsius. But if these fieldfares hadn't hopped the North Sea, these birds would be now experiencing the full force of a hyperborean winter – regularly dipping below minus 30 degrees in a landscape so harsh that in large parts of Scandinavia, even the wolves and elk will move south for the winter.

As soon as they arrive in Britain, fieldfares are desperate to refuel. Fortunately, they are not fussy, with one of the most varied diets of all thrushes. In the summer, inverte-brates are top of the menu. Come the autumn they switch to berries – drawing them into gardens across the country as they raid our hawthorns, rowans and cotoneasters. It's not unusual for a feeding flock to stay loyal to a single berry-laden tree while picking off every morsel. But as these run out come the winter, fieldfares seek out larger fruits, in sympathetically managed orchards where windfall is left. They can stay for months, until every rotting fruit is gone. And if these run out before they head home in early spring, they continue their road-trip of Britain's top restaurants. If things get really desperate, fieldfares can even be found searching for marine molluscs or other marine invertebrates along the coast.[2]

Sitting watching them, it is clear that the fieldfares are in control of the fallen fruit. Occasionally a blackbird will try to join the melee but is soon rebuffed by one of its larger cousins, often before it has even taken a mouthful. Relegated, the blackbirds resort to forming their own B-team. Under a nearby tree, ten are feeding together. Strongly territorial in our parks and gardens, it's unusual to see more than two or three in proximity. But here, the draw of the winter bounty leads to the formation of black-bird gangs. As hard as they try, they just don't seem capable of the strong social bonds that existed among the fieldfares, often fighting over the same apple when it is clear there were more than enough to go around.

Despite being the middle of winter, and with the last of the deciduous leaves well on their way through the diges-tive tracts of the orchard's abundant earthworms, many of the trees here still appear green with life. Mistletoe is unusual – an evergreen flowering plant capable of photo-synthesis, yet unable to survive without its host. In Britain, this parasitic plant favours broad-leaved trees such as lime, hawthorn, poplar and particularly, apple. Fittingly for the location of this orchard, mistletoe is the county flower of Herefordshire. While this is a fairly recent addition, its written history goes back much further.

At the time of his death in AD 79, Pliny the Elder had almost finished the first draft of his *Natural History*. His fastidious attention to detail ensured even the ancient Druidic ritual of oak and mistletoe was recorded. '*A priest arrayed in white vestments climbed the tree and, with a golden sickle, cuts down the mistletoe, which is caught in a white cloak.*' The next phase of this elaborate ceremony involves the sacrifice of two white bulls and prayers, with the mistletoe considered central in the creation of an elixir to cure infertility and poisoning. Thankfully, there doesn't appear to be any record of contemporary efforts to test its efficacy, but the roots of such a potion are likely related to the fact that the Celts believed that mistletoe berries were actually the semen of their thunder god – Taranis.

The Ancient Greek, Roman and Norse cultures also all held mistletoe as integral to various rituals and beliefs. While kissing under mistletoe is considered a Christmas custom today, the association between the winter equinox and mistletoe goes back to at least ancient Roman times. Between the 17th and the 23rd days of December, the Romans held their most important festival, Saturnalia; it was believed that hanging mistletoe above a doorway in this period would bring good fortune – and peace.

Here in the orchard, the weary branches buckling under the weight of mistletoe appear anything but fortunate. Even the lightest breeze leaves the orchard groaning as its mistletoe-laden limbs creak out a grumbling tune. There is an almost weekly switch between westerlies and northerlies in January – swinging the weather between the first hints of spring and the coldest days of winter. A powerful trill of clicks accompanies this grating chorus of heaving trees, the tell-tale of a true orchard specialist and one of its earliest breeding birds.

Mistle thrushes now sit alongside nightingales and turtle doves as one of Britain's fastest-declining species. They are charismatic inhabitants of our wood pastures, singing from and nesting in mature trees, yet gathering much of their food in open glades on the ground – and in the mistletoe of open-grown fruit trees. Mistle thrushes are both over-looked and vanishing in our countryside – but traditional orchards are as perfect a habitat as they can find.

These large thrushes may be a joy to see but can be infuriating to study. Firstly, they build incredibly *bad* nests. Easy to find, these regularly get predated. Secondly, after about five failed nests, they disappear for a month – only to reappear in May, taunting us with a contented brood of fledged chicks.

Despite the apparent inefficiency of the mistle thrush's nesting behaviour, it does actually appear to be part of their breeding strategy. Indeed, they haven't mirrored the national decline since we have been monitoring them here. Walking through the orchard after the New Year, I climb the slippery boughs, in an attempt to count up all of last year's nest efforts. Though mistle thrushes build their scruffy wool, hay and mud nests in as little as two days, these withstand the elements fairly well – so it's possible to find a dozen or so old nests in a January morning. These invariably have the characteristic signs of predation – a few fragments of broken turquoise eggshell sitting among a mess of shredded wool. A proven method is simply to walk around the orchard looking up into every fork or mistletoe clump; if there is any sign of sheep's wool – one of their favourite nest materials – there is a near certain chance that it's the remains of a mistle-thrush nest. Tying a piece of biodegradable marker tape below such sites reminds us of found nests, in the hope that it will make finding the upcoming year's nests a little easier in early March, when Ben and I start our breeding bird surveys, and licensed nest recording, for the British Trust for Ornithology.

Though named after it, mistle thrushes are by no means the only species to use mistletoe as a refuge. Over the past few years here, blackbirds, song thrushes, wood pigeons and particularly spotted flycatchers have all chosen dense clumps of mistletoe to raise their families in. Though it can be damaging in excess, mistletoe is a vital species – helping to provide winter fodder and summer shelter for the orchard's refugees.

In places like Scandinavia, Greenland and Alaska, it's not uncommon for a dense snow cover, or *subnivium*, to last for over six months at a time. But in most of Britain, it is rare for snow to settle on the ground for more than a few weeks. Even when it falls, it's business as usual for the rodents that call this ground layer home. If you sit and wait quietly in any orchard between October and April, before the vegetation has had a chance to build up again and there are still scraps of windfall fruit on the ground, you're likely to be rewarded with a sighting of one of the orchard's smallest mammals.

Bank voles are common – yet like many of our mammals, far from commonly seen. Similar to their field vole cousins, they have perfected the art of the shuffle-run. There is an easy difference, if you catch a glimpse of a rodent and wonder: mouse or vole? If it *skips*, it's a mouse. If it *shuffles*, it's a vole.

If you've ever played with a Scalextric set and hit stop-start-stop on your electric-powered micro-motor, this performs a near-perfect demonstration of how bank and field voles move through the undergrowth. These little bursts of activity allow the voles to avoid detection from the many predators that hunt them in the orchard. During the peak of the day, it's mainly field voles that are active, while the more nocturnal bank voles and mice stir to life as the light starts to fade. Now, they must avoid the attention of not one but four pairs of tawny owls that nest in the orchard's oldest apples, time-heavy oaks and sagging willows. In less than two months' time, female tawny owls will be incubating their eggs. To create the calcium supplies needed to do so, many hapless voles and mice will be ingested throughout the winter. January is a voracious month, where each of the orchard's inhabitants eats to excess as February, the most punitive of times, beckons fast.

By the end of January, the orchard is transformed. The first snow has brought with it the first wounds of winter. There really must be a snowflake that breaks the apple's back, as walking through Maze Orchard unveils a scene of destruction. Glacial but powerful, the weight of snow, accumulating on the mistletoe clumps, has proven too much for some. The frozen mass has acted as a giant lever, bringing some of our most loved veterans crashing to the ground.

An old Frederick cider apple, standing for perhaps sixty years, once held the most flawless form. Its trunk gave way at head-height to three thick and evenly-spaced branches. These then split again, symmetrically, as if controlled by the laws of mathematics as much as those of nature. Reaching it today, we can see the whole tree has been spliced open. Each of the main branches curves forlornly groundwards, acting as giant walking sticks for the central trunk. The limbs lie in symmetry to the last. Despite the damage, the central trunk stands resolute. If the frost doesn't soak into the new cracks, expanding and destroying from within, this tree just might survive.

Another old apple trunk, a magnificent Yarlington Mill, uprooted in a storm many years ago yet still clinging on, has finally succumbed. In 2016, a blackbird nested in its hollowing shell. The year before it hosted a wren. Now, its empty core lies split and dormant. But already, below the surface, the larvae of the rhinoceros beetle, even in the dead of winter, will be feasting on the dry rot within.

Towards the centre of this orchard, one fresh scar reveals the favourite nest cavity of a redstart. This pair had chosen exceptionally well. Their nest site was so well concealed behind a fold of deadwood that we had passed it many times – not believing such a tiny feature could conceal a nest. Now, their secret chamber has finally been revealed. It is surprising to see that the near-invisible cavity in fact extends more than a foot into the body of the tree. It doesn't appear to be the work of a woodpecker – the orchard's most likely excavator. Instead, over the years a slow combination of dry rot and invertebrate action likely created it.

In our increasingly sanitised green spaces – where rotten deadwood is hacked away before even beetles have a chance to find it – a dead tree is seen to be a useless thing. Yet the natural forces exercised by rot, fungi and beetles remain integral to the creation of dead wood in our adopted orchard – and to the diversity of its wildlife.

In Oak Orchard, too, the wreckage of winter is put on clear display. Despite being well outnumbered by fruit trees, the six giant English oak trees bisecting this, the largest of the three orchards, give it its name. The guardians of these pensioner pears and ageing apples, these oaks must be over three hundred years old – a good hundred years off their prime in a species that makes the giant tortoise appear as fleeting on our planet as a butterfly.

Now, just five oaks are standing. One of the giants has unexpectedly fallen. It lies exactly as it fell; a serene calm of smashed branches and scarred bark. Miraculously, an old Herefordshire Redstreak stands almost undamaged at the edge of the oak's crumbling crown, protected by its giant branches. A white rupture of crumbling sapwood contrasting against healthy yellow-white heartwood suggests that a fungal attack was responsible for this untimely death, likely working away at the roots until the tree could no longer support its huge bulk against relentless winter storms. Four tonnes of life has passed away – yet the orchard's fungal and beetle armies have already colonised this new barracks.

While a living oak can support over 350 species of insect – more than any other tree in Britain – half of that figure is made up of species using the decaying deadwood. In all, over 1,800 British invertebrates are reliant on decaying wood for their survival.[3] The volume of wood from this giant, slowly being eaten away by fungi and invertebrates, can take centuries to decompose. It creates a critical habitat for flora and fauna alike, while generating millions of mouthfuls of invertebrate prey across its decaying life.

The importance of deadwood such as this is hard to overstate. One third of all woodland birds nest in cavities. Two thirds of our bat species rely on tree holes for their winter and summer roosts. Deadwood has been identified as a crucial part of the carbon-capture cycle, and its slow release of nitrogen back into the environment helps regulate soil fertility. It's a sad sight losing such a magnificent tree – but it's reassuring to know that, resting in the orchard, this newly-deceased specimen might only be halfway through its useful life. This fallen giant will continue to support the orchard here for centuries to come.

Walking between these orchard trees – beaten into submission by the winter weather – is a seasonal reminder of the importance and ephemeral nature of deadwood. We seem obsessed with tidiness in the natural world, but the disorder and chaos here harbours life in abundance. When we try to remove this winter damage, we are stripping back a layer of key habitat. Deadwood is one of the raw materials feeding the biodiversity engine that makes our adopted orchard so special. This season is nature's inadvertent way of reminding us of the orchard's mortality – taking twigs, branches, limbs and sometimes whole trees as it sees fit. And the orchard will receive many more fresh wounds, before the winter is out.

FEBRUARY

THE SOUND OF TREES

BEN

*You learn that if you sit down in
the woods and wait, something happens.*

HENRY DAVID THOREAU

February in the Malverns is the coldest month of the
year. As you arrive, very early in the morning, and tuck
yourself quietly at the base of one of the open-grown oaks,
the tops of the orchard's tallest trees lie hidden in the
freezing mist. Under such conditions, something eerie
happens to the orchard. The trees, it seems, begin to talk.

They begin drumming to one another. Different branches,
each with a different tenor, begin to reverberate. Their
sounds – hollow, brittle, machine-gun loud and right above
your head – bounce around the orchard, amplified in the
mist. You can, for a fanciful moment, picture yourself in a

scene from *The Lord of the Rings*, where ancient Ents hold long meetings to discuss the future of their kind. The hail of staccato gunfire goes on for half an hour or more, as if some battle is being fought high in the invisible boughs above your head. And in many ways, that is exactly what is happening. Woodpeckers, the unseen drummers in this battle, are gearing up for war.

The loudest culprit is the great spotted woodpecker, firing off volleys of sharp, half-second drumming bursts that fade rapidly in tone. Great spots appear almost demonically possessed as the winter fades. Sometimes, a few gentle taps of a stick against an oak trunk is enough to bring a supercharged male bounding in overhead, uttering his angry *'kek'* call to let you know who is in charge of this particular grove of Tom Putt cider apples.

Longer, quieter and more mechanical in tone, the faster, brittle drilling of the lesser spotted woodpecker is a more cautious overture. Perhaps once, or twice, as the drumming contest rages, the sparrow-sized male, and female, both of whom drum, may decide to open fire. On many mornings, however, they remain completely silent.

A lot of literature states that green woodpeckers do not drum. In this orchard, we've found they often do – but it's a very underwhelming affair. A feeble rattle of slower contacts with a large, dead branch fizzles out as soon as it's begun. Instead the green woodpecker has its famous 'yaffle', a piercingly clear laugh that, coupled with a show of red and green, renders the male every bit as alluring to females of his species. Violent concussion is not for everyone, it seems.

Indeed, on first inspection, drumming by woodpeckers is one of nature's 'impossible' phenomena. If we attempted to hit our heads against wood up to twenty-two times in a second, we would be concussed long before reaching this stage. A sudden deceleration of 100 g (gravitational force) generally leaves our species out for the count. Repeating such strange behaviour would, over a protracted period of lessons not being learned, result in brain damage. And when we come home from an unproductive office meeting and describe it as being 'like knocking your head against a wall', we unsurprisingly forget that not every animal family feels the same way about voluntary head contact with a hard surface. Woodpeckers, however, pull off their head-banging party trick hundreds of times in a morning, over dozens of mornings in succession across the territorial months of February, March and April – with no ill-effects whatsoever. The solution lies in the world's most sophisticated shock-absorbing technology.

Four secrets allow woodpeckers to do what other species cannot. Spongy bones, acting as a shield, absorb damaging vibrations; preventing them reaching from the woodpecker's bill into its brain. Rather than the brain meeting the inner confines of the skull, it too is separated by a vibration-damping reservoir known as cerebrospinal fluid. The *hyoid*, a solid yet elasticated support for the tongue, distributes the load from the vibration. Lastly, a woodpecker's bill is extremely strong, and does not bend or fracture. I have, over the years, seen a number of species, including sparrowhawks and smaller birds such as blackbirds, with not only deformed but broken bills. To this day, I have never seen a woodpecker with an inch of damage to its bill, and I doubt that many people have. In all, the woodpecker's combined shock-absorbing armoury allows it to experience a colossal deceleration of 1200 g – and go about its daily business of warning off rivals without a hangover headache the morning after.[1]

Traditional organic orchards, with standing dead trees, provide all three of Britain's woodpeckers with the ideal conditions for survival: a maze of soft-wooded, insect-rich trees, where grubs squirm below the bark. Flaky apple wood in dead snags provides the perfect nesting site for the spotted woodpeckers, while the green makes its home most often in the dead timber within the apple trunk itself. For the green woodpecker, too, the verdant grasslands between the orchard trees are rich in its favoured yellow meadow ants.

As a result, our adopted orchard is home to at least three pairs of green woodpeckers, at least five pairs of great spotted woodpeckers and, each year, at least one, sometimes two pairs of the nationally-precious lesser spotted wood-peckers. Each spring, just before and after sunrise, the orchard gunfire salute provides a memorable chorus, the more so because its frenzied participants are most often lost within the orchard's cloud world.

So dense are the February fogs that you can sometimes see no more than a few metres in front of you. Birds loom as giants. The size of tiny goldcrests or blue tits appears greatly exaggerated; a buzzard drifting over the apples calls to mind some enormous eagle from prehistoric times. Quite how dense fog has such an effect on size perception I don't know, but without any sense of colour, objects appear to take on a size far greater than their own. Here, you also become drawn into the myriad shapes of this veteran forest – and the ancient stories of its trees.

From the mountains of deadwood left over from the winter, to the standing dead trees; from the bee-hives to the lack of chemical application for over fifty years, Nancy and David have maintained this veteran Eden as both a viable cider orchard and a wood pasture whose richness eclipses that of many conservation woodlands. From them, we have come to inherit a privileged understanding of quite how rare and unique the orchard's woodlands are – and quite how precious its living history.

Since at least 1840, tithe records show that an orchard has grown on this site. The age of the hop kiln, built around 1720, suggests a great deal longer. Due to the painstaking choices made by its owners, this is now a cider orchard. For decades, many varieties of apples and pears, some now lost entirely to the countryside at large, have been cherished and protected.

Of the orchard's seven hundred standing fruit trees, most of the veteran pear trees stand in Hop Kiln Orchard. This is part of a far wider fruit forest, now largely lost in history. In the orchards from Much Marcle north to the regions of Colwall and Mathon in the Malverns, orchard historians have found the greatest concentration of old pear varieties anywhere in Britain. Perhaps, given our intense history of cultivation and fruit creation, there are more pear breeds surviving here, overlooked in this landscape, than anywhere on Earth. The thirty veteran pears that remain, limbs splitting at angles like a three-pronged fork, preserve an encrypted story that few alive can now read.

Most of these pears are Thorn pears. Of all the orchard's breeds, the Thorn is the most stable provider of a balanced perry come the autumn months. Several others are Moorcrofts. The perry from this pear is used not only for drinking, but to wash the Stinking Bishop cheese, adding to its distinctive taste. This not only enriches the flavour, but heightens the smell. In spite of these impressive pear stands, which every year host nesting treecreepers, redstarts and hornets, three other pears in the orchard are worthy of special attention.

In Maze Orchard stands the orchard's oldest fruiting tree. At 150 years old, the Barland looks deader than most dead trees. Fissured by time, it bends outwards, more lateral than vertical, like a child's broken catapult. It seems unfathomable how it survives, yet each year, perfect Barland pears hang from its branches. In Hop Kiln Orchard, however, we find two of the rarest trees in the English countryside. A Flakey-Bark, whose apples seem irresistible to badgers, stretches proudly through the mist; a craggy giant known only from a few locations. And in the far corner stands the Betty Prosser pear.

So rare is her kind that until her discovery, only twelve were known to exist, all of them around the remote orchard village of Corse, in Gloucestershire.[2] This previously unknown tree makes number thirteen. Come September, the stalks of the Betty Prosser give it away: petrified flamingo necks – pink, arched hangers clasping the pear to the tree. Rarer than a Siberian tiger or Amur leopard, no one, except her attentive owners, notices Betty's silent struggle for survival. Yet unlike the orchard's apples, which can break loose in the heavy clay soil, her sturdy roots, like many of her pear kindred, are standing firm – and she puts forth fruit every year.

Betty's furrowed bark is, even in late winter, a focus of attention for gleaners and foragers. Treecreepers spend much time here inspecting the old pears, curved bills probing every crumpled inch not only for tiny invertebrates but for future nesting cavities. Pear bark peels away from the living tree rather well, and treecreepers, like bats, can squeeze into the most infinitesimal of gaps. The central trunk is riven with the successive homes of green woodpeckers; a strange apartment block where, each year, the woodpeckers excavate new holes to avoid infestations of mites building up in last year's summer home. In most years, noctule bats call her cavernous internal spaces home. But Betty is useful not only to the orchard's thriving cavity dwellers. Come autumn, the deep orange perry from her fruits makes her more than an idle piece of history. She is, perhaps, a fragile reminder of how we once cultivated fruits with the same care, and skill, that the French still use to cultivate their vineyards.

The pears form fascinating statues in the winter mists. But with little ability to see, I now turn my attention to the health of the apples, and how they have braved the onslaught of wet soils, frosts and driving winds that so often prove the downfall of the orchard giants. To my immense relief, the Old Kingston Black has survived another winter. This is our very favourite orchard tree; a sentiment shared by its owners. While most cider apples are either too sweet, too sharp or possess too many tannins, which can render them acerbic and dry in the extreme, the Kingston provides a famously well-balanced cider. Standing for seventy years, it is a living ecosystem. Its limbs splay at the bottom, creating a moss-encrusted cave. Here, in the warm, moist caverns of its roots, strange wonders lie. From late winter onwards, from within its glistening dark wood, *Stemonitopsis typhina*, a cobalt-coloured slime mould, carpets the base of the Old Kingston like a coral forest transplanted from the bottom of the sea. If lying underwater, you would almost expect to find clownfish swimming among these lurid fronds, so utterly out of place do they seem in the orchard's sepia winter.

Slime moulds are not fungi; they can freely live as single cell organisms, aggregating to form reproductive structures. When food is in short supply, they move as an eerie wave across the rotting forest floor, consuming micro-organisms within the surface of dead wood. While the Old Kingston is very much alive, parts of its heartwood are now decaying. The translucent, glutinous corals gnawing at Old Kingston's feet are *sporangia*, spore capsules that will rapidly mature. In just a few days, this eerie gelatine forest, nestled within a single apple tree, will mutate, as the slime mould's spores are released. Then, the dramatic fruiting bodies will vanish, as new, walled spores delve into the apple's timber. Here, their actions will not kill the tree but keep it alive.

50

Squirming and squelching across Old Kingston's venerable limbs, the creeping slime mould soup will root out and consume millions of bacteria within the wood.

Old Kingston's limbs are so rich in deadwood, in feeding opportunities, and the ground below so rank with winter's rotten fruit, that we have to date recorded forty bird species within his spacious grasp. Jackdaws, goldfinches, mistle thrushes, redstarts and rhinoceros beetles are just some of the orchard's denizens who have called his cavernous comfort home. But Old Kingston is not the only special tree.

By no means every breed of apple tree can be recognised in its winter state. Only in early autumn will its fruits give it away. But Strawberry Normans are distinct at any time of year. Proud lateral limbs stretch horizontally like a gnarled embrace. The Normans are particularly favoured by the orchard's small insectivores. Here, marsh tits from the hazel hedge, nuthatches from Oak Orchard and hazel dormice have all been watched, at different times of year, traversing its expansive limbs.

Equally distinctive, by virtue of the knobbled carbuncle growths on its tortured branches, is the Blenheim Orange. Discovered close to Oxford's Blenheim Palace as long ago as 1740, this is one of the orchard's many fruit-bearing migrants. According to one Herefordshire cookery book, the apples create 'a noble sauce of legendary repute'.[3] Yet like so much of our culinary heritage, the magnificent taste of the Blenheim Orange has been all but forgotten. In its carbuncles lie epicormic growths; the tree's response to damage or stress, as it pushes out new shoots from buds dormant below the bark. This apple has yet to wake up from its winter slumber, but clambering up it I find, concealed, the tennis-ball moss-green nest of a chaffinch. An ungainly slither up to the next storey, and the frost-latticed threads of an old spotted flycatcher home nestle within a deep knot in the trunk.

Like the pears, many of the apples we have come to know are bucolic refugees in the modern countryside. While their fruits were once famous, and they once grew at the heart of a thriving farming operation, most of these ancient breeds have been grubbed and forgotten. The Colwall Quoining, famous for its angular apples, is endemic to this small postage stamp of the Earth's surface. The Newland Sack, a Herefordshire breed dating back to 1800, and recorded in the *Pomona*, has virtually vanished from the Malvern landscape. Its taste, however, is super-lative; a rich dessert apple of intense sweetness. Here too grow the Stoke Edith Pippin, the Ten Commandments and the orchard's most versatile performer, the ancient Tom Putt. Raised in the 1700s by a Reverend of this name, it can produce not only culinary apples, but apple juice and cider.[4]

As little known as these apple breeds is the history of how they came here. Farmers' wives in the eighteenth century would often bring with them to their new husband's orchard a selection of favoured apple breeds[5] – and so the orchard's diversity has grown not only from culinary but marital choice. Likewise, orchard workers of the eighteenth century were often paid, in part, in cider. They were there-fore permitted to exercise great preference as to which cider they drank. Their choices, too, are reflected in the fog-filled monoliths around.

Even as the air warms, the mist lies so thick on many trees that sound becomes the only guide. The orchard choristers make life harder still as they bounce song between the boughs. One master ventriloquist is the mistle thrush. In the month or so before nest-building, in early February, it is the haunting song of mistle thrushes – sad blackbirds lamenting their vanishing world – that carries through the freezing fog long after the woodpecker gunfire has died down.

If you hear a dry rattling call from a mistle thrush, and the bird is perhaps ten metres away or more, the chances are you are actually very close to where it has chosen to nest. For years, however, we didn't realise this, and followed instead the sound of the birds. In all probability, that was exactly what they wanted us to do.

The songs and calls of the orchard's birds appear most alike if they share a similar portion of this jostling world. Nuthatches and lesser spotted woodpeckers are most often seen sneaking through the tall, dead branches in the high crowns of the orchard oaks. Both have a *'kee-kee-kee'* call that carries for well over a hundred metres. Most often, after dawn, the only way to find a lesser spotted woodpecker is to follow its 'muffled kestrel' calls through the apples. These calls appear designed to carry far, but rarely do they pinpoint the singer moving nimbly through the canopy.

Deeper down, weaving between the dense groves of old

apples and pears, comes the laugh of the green woodpecker. This is a bird that should stand out a mile, but like other birds sporting green, yellow and red, such as our now vanished golden orioles, they are, it seems, aware of this fact – and fuse into the greens of the orchard underworld. Green woodpeckers spend much time low down, tucked against trunks. Often, as soon as they have 'yaffled', they depart, bounding away through the orchard. They move incessantly around their rotting kingdom, and seldom call anywhere close to their nest. Even though their nest holes, tunnels deep into the trunk, are obvious once you stumble on them, it can take many hours of being laughed at before you get anywhere close to finding a green woodpecker's home.

Other colourful birds, such as jays, prove remarkably elusive in the orchard maze. Their short, sharp barks, like the rattle of the mistle thrush, tell other birds that the orchard's best nest-robber is in town, but then the call stops – and leaves the watcher with no clue at all. Many hours of careful tree-by-tree searching, come April, will discover the nests of jays stashed deep in mistletoe or ivy. One, on inspection, is lined entirely with what appears to be a single ball of red string.

Each year, in late winter and early spring, the orchard's singers play a dual game. Birds are better heard and not seen, and so each utters cryptic traces of music; the bars of incomplete melodies. Advertise too little, and nobody finds or fears you. Advertise too boldly, and you give too much away. Much fieldwork in woodland derives from interpreting, and chasing, these fractured, cautious melodies.

*

The orchard song becomes more complex when deceit comes into play. A chorus of angry jays and mistle thrushes in an old pear has twice yielded the sight of a tawny owl being ignominiously mobbed from its roosting cavity, flopping in resignation across the orchard, carefully escorted by jays, like winged bouncers removing a particularly difficult customer. But jays, which have shared their homes with tawny owls for thousands of years, have also learned to mimic owls.

On one occasion, I watched a pair of carrion crows approach an area where a jay had concealed its nest. At this moment, both the crows and myself were totally thrown when a tawny owl began hooting in the middle of the day. On closer inspection, the hooting was, in fact, feigned by the male jay, some way from the nest, whereas the female, as far as I could make out, was still tucked up incubating eggs. In the end, my feeling was that the crows were more baffled by the jay's general commotion than fearful of an owl. Their expressions, in my mind, read 'we can see you – you're extremely obvious, pink and blue – you're certainly not an owl and you're definitely a jay'. Yet the nest defence was successful nonetheless, and the crows never, to my knowledge, found that particular jays' nest. The use of mimicry by jays, clever as they are, is clearly not yet as advanced as that of some African birds such as honeyguides or drongos. For example, writing in *British Birds*, the naturalist Connor Jameson describes similar tactics being used by jays, against both magpies and carrion crows. In summary, he writes that he 'saw no evidence it was having a deterrent effect'.[6] Pink, blue and very loud, it appears there is room for improvement for jays if they are to fool their crow cousins in the future evolutionary arms race of the orchard.

Perhaps jays could take lessons from starlings, the orchard's undisputed master mimics. Starlings, wheezing away at the start of spring, can insert into their guttural, bubbling songs remarkable passages of redstart and nuthatch, buzzard and mistle thrush, to name but a few. They can and will again deceive us completely. Being originally adapted to living amid hundreds of different bird species, the natural mimicry of the starling has grown to encompass an average repertoire of fifteen to twenty distinct imitations – but why?

So far, nobody knows. The ecologist Andrew Hindmarsh has studied such mimicry in depth. Of all possible reasons for mimicry in starlings, the theory still being entertained is that successful imitation, and therefore a more elaborate song, may further sexual selection.[7] Another hypothesis is that mimicry simply expresses 'mistakes' acquired during song learning, but that does not cut it for Nick or me. The significant time spent watching a starling repeat, perfectly, the notes of a song thrush, suggests something more deliberate. There is, of course, an alternative explanation, increasingly used to explain 'flippant' behaviour in creatures from dolphins to chimpanzee – that is, that starlings are simply having fun. But for now, all we have been able to ascertain beyond doubt is that starlings are able to fool us on a very regular basis.

What is becoming forgotten in many parts of Britain, however, is the orchard song itself. Since the 1970s, Britain has lost three out of every four of our lesser spotted woodpeckers. Starlings in our woodlands have largely vanished, retreating in ever-diminishing flocks to an ever-smaller number of our towns. And a host of other birds that still flourish here, from bullfinches to marsh tits, spotted flycatchers to cuckoos, are all in terminal decline.[8]

Those who, like us, have heard the orchard song will never forget it. Its vigour and fierce, layered melodies we will remember forever. But the orchard song grows quieter each year.

MARCH

PERIL IN PARADISE

NICK

It was one of those March days when the sun shines hot and the wind blows cold: when it is summer in the light, and winter in the shade.

CHARLES DICKENS

The crime scene is fresh. Clearly there was a struggle; the remains appear to be some distance from the initial blow. The perpetrator has made little effort to cover their tracks. Evidence lies scattered. Less than fifty metres away is a second victim – showing all the same traits: an open patch of ground, cleanly plucked feathers, no body. Over the past few weeks, this has become a regular occurrence. Some of the victims are woodpigeons and magpies, but even more striking is a regular number of pheasants. A serial killer is working in the orchard – and no one has dared bring it to the dock.

We start by working through the most common ground predators. While they would be able to tackle a wood pigeon, it is rare for a fox, polecat, badger or stoat to take down a healthy bird. Yet mammals can always surprise. A few years ago, one courageous weasel made the national papers after being photographed hitching a ride on the back of a green woodpecker,[1] presumably catching the ground-feeding bird off guard before attempting to over-power it with a bite to the neck. The green woodpecker – known for the strong neck muscles that it uses to prise open ant mounds – decided otherwise, taking off in panic with the adult weasel clasped to its back. While one weasel's derring-do *almost* resulted in a meal, the power of flight as a rule eludes this group of mammals.

Tellingly, there is another clue that points the finger firmly back to our feathered friends. No mammal species plucks its prey with such finesse; one clipped breast feather at a time. And this leaves only three likely culprits in the regular birdlife of our adopted orchard. The identity parade line-up consists of tawny owl, buzzard – and sparrowhawk.

The first would seem an unusual suspect. As well as feasting on the abundant rodents of the orchard, tawny owls have the most varied diet of all our island's owl species. When Ben and I met on the popular BBC series *Springwatch*, one of our first jobs was the twelve-hour nocturnal surveil-lance of the broadcast's many live cameras. We were in luck. One of our charges was a delightfully plump little tawny owl that earned the nickname 'Grub'. Over the course of three weeks, we watched as Grub's attentive parents brought him everything from slugs to slow worms

– and once, a moorhen! The tawny owl's ability to exploit such a wide variety of prey – they've even been caught catching goldfish from garden ponds – is one of the reasons that tawny owls are the most widespread of Britain's owl species.[2] However, despite their will to kill, the crime scene didn't seem quite right for tawny owls. For starters, it's not widely known for tawnies to pluck their prey on the ground.

Then there were two. You rarely spend more than a few hours in the orchard without hearing the sharp '*kree, eeee*' of a patrolling buzzard. Occasionally, as we sit tucked up against a fallen tree, watching winter migrants fight over the apples, or trying to pin down a new nest site, a buzzard will drop down below the canopy and glide silently through the orchard just a couple of metres above the ground to surprise the apple gluttons. But buzzards rarely get far before the mob arrives.

The orchard has a plentiful jackdaw population. As soon as they see or hear a buzzard, a cacophony erupts, as the squadron scrambles from the oldest fruit trees and sets about the aerial bombardment of their foe. This is a game of Russian roulette, with very live ammunition. We have seen a buzzard here pirouette in mid-air and come crashing down on top of an inexperienced jackdaw; a novice recruit to the mobbing brigade yet to master the aerial prowess required to escape such a powerful hunter. But while the buzzards can't be ruled out, it is the presence of the dead magpies that shines the light firmly on what we conclude is our final suspect. Buzzards occasionally take crows and jackdaws, but it's rarer for them to target magpies with such regularity.

A female sparrowhawk, however, is an extraordinary killer. She punches well above her weight. With such a long tail, magpies are relatively slow fliers. Easily outpaced by a pursuing hawk, they rely on intelligence and teamwork to avoid attack. While towards the top end of a sparrow-hawk's capabilities, the orchard's black-and-white mafia are far from invulnerable. Once pinned to the ground, magpies can indeed fall prey to this most agile of orchard hunters. Sparrowhawks have even been shown to drown magpies by pinning their heads beneath the surface of watery pools.

The sparrowhawk is arguably the most adaptable of Britain's birds of prey; flourishing from Hyde Park in Central London to the remotest gardens of the Outer Hebrides. Perfectly adapted to hunting among trees, these airborne hand grenades are primed to explode through the smallest of gaps. Surprising their victims with a final forwards sally of talons, sparrowhawks can even dig small birds from deep within the cover of the densest bushes. The renowned ornithologist Professor Ian Newton explains how sparrow-hawks use no fewer than *seven* different hunting strategies, with names such as 'contour-hugging in flight' and 'short-stay perch-hunting'.[3] The result is a ruthlessly efficient hunter; equally capable of plucking a swallow chick from the underside of a barn joist as taking out a magpie in a stooping attack. Yet even a sparrowhawk, we thought, would struggle to regularly ambush birds as large as pheasants.

One day, as Ben and I headed once more to the crime scene of Maze Orchard, we caught sight of a pair of birds, high overhead. A wing's distance apart, they glided in concentric circles up on a thermal. We cautiously mumbled '*sparrowhawks* . . .?' to one another, while waiting for a better view. But this parallel flying was only the warm-up to the main event. At the top of their routine, the smaller bird tipped on one wing, rotating a full 180 degrees to lock talons with the larger. On this cue, both birds arched their wings back and allowed themselves to stall, commencing a free-falling downward pirouette as they made no effort to slow their descent. Just when it looked like their tangled parachute would end in a headlong collision with the woodland canopy below, they broke apart.

As these supple dancers flew across the treeline, they afforded us a few seconds to get a clearer look. Long, elastic wings generating slow and deliberate deep wingbeats, a long tail pitched with bold white covert feathers where it joined the body, and a noticeably protruding head glowed with fierce red eyes. Muscles bulged from every airborne sinew. 'Goshawks!' Ben exhaled, in a tone somewhere between excitement and disbelief.

We had chanced upon front row seats to a prime British natural history spectacle – the pair-bonding display of northern goshawks, as they worked hard to test each other's strength, agility and endurance. In stunned silence, we enjoyed another five minutes of slow flapping, tail fanning and displaying before the birds completed one last high flight, pitched, and bolted head first down into the woodland. Here, over the coming months, we would discover their nest, placed deep in the ivy of an oak; proof that in spite of some textbooks' assertions that this species needs large forests, goshawks are just as at home in copses of deciduous trees. While goshawks choose to nest in shaded canopies, they prefer rides and open woodlands in which to hunt. The orchard was thus an ideal killing field for one of Britain's deadliest assassins. The mystery of the pheasants was resolved: goshawks can kill large geese without a second thought.

The case file was closed. We did not have one assassin after all. We had a pair – and they were holding territory adjacent to the fruit trees. This added a whole new dimension to the orchard's biodiversity. Once a common woodland predator, intense persecution saw to their effective extinction in Britain by the end of the nineteenth century. Thanks to deliberate releases by falconers and immigration from Scandinavian populations,[4] they are now recovering well in most of the heavily-wooded counties of our island.

The presence of goshawks in an orchard is, perhaps counter-intuitively, the most welcome of news for its smallest songbirds. Goshawks rarely bother with such tiny protein parcels, yet are remorseless hunters of jays, jackdaws, crows and magpies – four of the main nest-robbers in the orchard. Given any chance, goshawks go further. They will destroy adult sparrowhawks and buzzards. We have even, on one occasion, found the remains of a freshly plucked tawny owlet, scattered below an active owl nest in an old, split white willow. By feasting on the large, goshawks allow the smallest to thrive.

So powerful and feared is the goshawk that entire species depend on its ferocity for their own survival. Our adopted orchard's red-eyed furies would help keep predator numbers at a natural balance; winged gamekeepers whose brood depended on the task. All of the crow family here, even the ravens, would have to keep on their guard. All were now firmly on the menu.

The orchard's case file hasn't always proven so hard to crack. A couple of years ago, we came across a coal tit nest tucked deep in the limb of a pear. The coal tit's habit of nesting among tangled networks of old roots makes the base of the oldest fruit trees, bursting loose from their clay soil, a natural place for them to raise a family. The coal tit's subtle little call can easily be mistaken for some part of a blue or great tit's repertoire – but they have a fairly catchy 'go home, go home, go home' that stands out. This pair's behaviour at the nest – irregular visits by a single bird – highlighted that they were still incubating, so two weeks later we headed back up to try and uncover the life history of this rather understudied species.

Watching the nest, however, we could not see the clockwork-like routine of busy tit parents. In fact, we couldn't see any activity at all. As we cautiously approached the nest, Ben and I paused, and then looked at one another in baffled amazement. The oval entrance to the coal tit's nest site was completely *blocked*. A small, golden-brown head was poking out, jet black eyes bulging from their sockets. Limp oversized ears and drooping whiskers emphasised that this unfortunate wood mouse was extremely dead.

Inspecting further, it appeared there was only one possible scenario that could have ended in such a dire result. This strongly arboreal omnivore must have chanced upon the coal tits' nest, scared off the adult incubating bird and then proceeded to scoff all the eggs in the cavity. A coal tit lays on average between nine and ten eggs.[5] If our greedy wood mouse ate them all, he would likely have eaten around fourteen calories, equivalent to *half* of his own weight. This would have meant that, on trying to leave the nest, our mouse got very, very stuck.

Winnie the Pooh famously experienced a similar fate one afternoon, while visiting his friend Rabbit. Having eaten Rabbit's entire supply of honey, portly Pooh got wedged in the entrance hole to his host's underground home. Rabbit – pragmatic as ever – decided to hang tea towels on the hapless Pooh Bear's rear end. After a few days' forced fasting, and an awful lot of effort, the young bear was freed from his ordeal. For our wood mouse, however, the ending was far from a happy one. Yet here was natural selection in action. Death by stupidity wins no points in the race to further one's species – let alone in the competitive world of the orchard.

Few species have the odds stacked against them here more than Britain's 'flying pompoms'. Without their extraordinary tail, long-tailed tits would be top of the podium as Britain's smallest bird. But what they lack in size they certainly make up for in attitude; a party of long-tailed tits on a bird feeder can fiercely hold their own against much larger competitors.

To grow such a bullish team, they must first successfully fledge a family. This starts with the finest of nest-building skills, as these tiny tailors carefully weave over six thousand pieces of spider silk, lichen, moss and feathers into a tapered cocoon.[6] Lining the inside with feathers (they're not fussy, they'll even pluck from roadkill) and the outside with camouflaged lichen, the end product appears as a miniature insulated sleeping bag hanging upright within their fortress of bramble, holly or gorse. As has happened in the past four years, a careful inspection of the hedge-line in Hop Kiln Orchard yields a perfectly-built long-tailed tit nest within a thick clump of holly and bramble.

Despite all this effort, only a fifth of nests avoid predation. For those lucky ones that make it, fledging is a comical affair. The whole nest begins to wriggle and bulge at the seams, straining at the mossy hooks and silken loops. Eventually, a head appears; except it's often *not* from the entrance hole. The excitement of fledging day in an over-crowded sarcophagus simply overcomes the natural Velcro, as the first eager youngster makes a break for freedom. This process can repeat itself over a dozen times, as an often scarcely believable number of chicks rupture out of what appears to be a tiny silken chamber; the Mary Poppins' bag of the natural world – where each surprise is yet another long-tailed tit chick.

However, for those that don't succeed, their breeding season isn't over. Unlike almost every other British species, if long-tailed tits fail at their own nest, they will often seek out one of their family members and go and help *them* rear their brood. Using call as a measure of relatedness, they particularly look for the nest of a male relative. Genetically, if you can't rear your own offspring – which you're 50 per cent related to – it makes sense to help rear a relative's offspring which you might be 25 per cent related to, rather than none at all. As a result, around half of all nests end up with a helper – markedly improving the number of young that fledge.[7] And next year, and the year after that, the long-tailed tits will most likely return to their holly fortress, halfway down the Hop Kiln Orchard hedge.

Hidden between peeling deadwood and lightning-scarred cracks, or sometimes deep underground, the first bees and butterflies are starting to stir. While a few will take wing as early as January, the majority will be waiting for the perfect combination of temperature and day-length to trigger sensory receptors – their biological weather stations – that tell them it is time to wake from their winter slumbers. The nectar provided by early-blossoming trees and other March flowers is a lifeline for these early risers. One March day, Ben and I were lucky enough to see this in action. Peeling back a side-plate-sized piece of bark, so that we could place a new nest box flush against one of the older trees, revealed a small tortoiseshell butterfly, wings closed and motionless. A centimetre of bark seemed a meagre shelter from a cold British winter – but it had clearly worked. Four of its six feet delicately pinched the wood, having bound it to this coarse texture since the autumn. Dappled underwings cryptically concealed against the bark, it remained perfectly stationary: a still-life painting apparently unaware of its rude awakening. Deciding that it wasn't quite ready to awaken, we returned the bark, sealing its stowaway back into welcome darkness.

This was obviously enough of a cue for the butterfly, for on this movement, it flashed open its wings – the brightest orange in the orchard. Blacks, whites and startling blues lit up its surroundings momentarily: the Jekyll to this apparently dull butterfly's Hyde. After ten minutes spent familiarising itself, the butterfly alighted and flew off among the bare orchard trees, fledging for the second and final time in its life.

The tortoiseshell's first flight into the world would have taken place in the previous June. Upon emerging from its chrysalis – a cryptic casket of leafy brown and sharp, serrated edges; as easily overlooked as a dead leaf – it would have spent the rest of the summer and autumn building up fat reserves before scouting nearby cavities and cracks for a place to overwinter. This one, like many of its ancestors before it, had chosen a peeling layer of bark to nestle in behind. Now awake, it will spend the next two months searching for a mate. After eleven months – just 1 per cent of the lifespan of a veteran apple tree – this small tortoiseshell's fleeting existence in the orchard will be over.

On a visit at the end of the month, Ben and I decided to check the jackdaw colony in the middle of Hop Kiln Orchard. These aged Strawberry Norman apples are some of the orchard's oldest; a dozen trees, all sagging at the end of their life. Some appear to be almost all deadwood, yet each spring the odd sprig of green growth hints that they're not ready to surrender just yet. Knotted and twisted limbs, shaped by decades of pruning, parasitic mistletoe and woodpecker excavations, are now pitted with holes. Entering these hollows reveals rotted out caverns, where heartwood once grew to feed these mighty specimens. But today, these empty cores still generate life. Stuffed with sticks, most of the deep cavities in this ageing apple stand have been adopted by a pair of jackdaws.

Throughout March, each of the monogamous pairs takes time to reaffirm their bond – performing in-flight cartwheels to impress one another. They also 'allopreen' – a term meaning *'you scratch my back and I'll scratch yours'*. Colonies will often execute these aerial routines en masse. Jackdaws are highly intelligent and extremely good at recognising one another. This helps them identify who to look out for in *their* colony.

Next comes a spot of spring-cleaning. Without regular maintenance, parasites can quickly build up. Lice, ticks and fleas can all be fatal to young chicks. There is a nest in one of the old farm barns here that is at least three metres deep – the result of decades of building and renovation work by successive pairs of jackdaws. Selecting fresh twigs, the birds re-line the perimeter of the nest to create a new nest bowl. Once complete, they head over to the small flock of Soay sheep in the neighbouring fields, and carefully gather up wool. They'll often hop up onto the back of a ruminating ewe, gain a firm purchase with two feet locked into the animal's rump fleece, and carefully pull out fresh clumps of wool to carry back to their nests. The sheep are unfazed by such thievery: a welcome thinning of their heavy winter coats.

Nest-building is a charming time to watch jackdaws, though if they spot you, after a couple of alarm calls, the whole colony will simply flee: birds scrambling to eject from their own nest holes for fear of being trapped inside by a predator. Those in deeper holes sometimes sit it out, eyeballing us from deep in their nest chambers as we inspect each for eggs, as part of our work for the BTO's Nest Records Scheme. Peering into these cavities is not for the timorous; a pair of monochrome yellow-grey eyes looming suddenly out of the darkness can rattle even the most composed observer.

And that is precisely how on this March visit, we found a most unusual nest. Jackdaw eggs are fairly distinctive – a wonderful pale turquoise flecked with black pen strokes. Yet nestled among the five turquoise eggs was one crisp, tapered ping-pong-ball-size *cream* egg. We were stumped. There are few species that produce eggs like this, and even fewer that nest in the orchard. What was most unusual was that if the egg was present *before* the jackdaws started laying, they almost certainly would have predated it – jackdaws are adept egg thieves. Yet this egg seemed to have slipped in under the radar and had been accepted by the incubating birds.

It only dawned upon us what we had witnessed when, close by a little later in the year, we discovered a mandarin duck's nest, with twelve identical cream eggs, nestled among a halo of fine down feathers, in one of our tawny owl nest boxes. Ducks, and specifically the cavity-nesting ducks, are prolific egg dumpers; a strategy they use to quite literally prevent all their eggs from being put in one, downy basket. Quite why our mandarin mother had chosen a jackdaw nest we'll never know, but her urge to lay additional eggs had clearly overridden any ability of hers to recognise an even vaguely suitable host.

Sadly, when we returned to check up on the fate of our mystery egg, there were five jackdaw chicks growing well – but no sign of the outcast. It was a risky strategy, but perhaps our egg donor succeeded in finding another mandarin nest to deposit other eggs in with more success.

We think of this orchard's endless cavities and nooks as a jumbled Dickensian dwelling, where different parents and their families trip continually over one another. We think of its story as not unlike that great author's novels, where, through happenstance or strange design, the varied lives of a city's inhabitants smash together – with improbable results. By spring, all of the orchard's many stories begin to intertwine. Here lies a tangled world where carpenters and singers, lovers and murderers jostle side by side.

As March comes to a close, the whole of the orchard begins to take on a new tune. The hum of the bees is returning, and it won't be long before the first of the spring migrants return to their natal trees in search of their own mates for the busy nesting season. The orchard has delivered a suite of surprises. But it has many more secrets yet to share.

APRIL

OF BUILDERS AND BEES

NICK

April . . . Hath put a spirit of youth in every thing.

WILLIAM SHAKESPEARE

A new member has joined the orchard chorus. Walking through the apple maze, a persistent *'tlack-tlack'* echoes around the trees. I move a short distance, pause, and carefully scan the direction from which the noise came. And then, *'tlack-tlack'* – it's behind me! Are there two? I try to glimpse the call's owner; pinning it down to a few clumps of mistletoe within an old pear. *'Tlack-tlack'*. The sound mimics the metal marbles in a Newton's cradle. My suspicions are roused – this is not a bird that has been seen in the orchard this year.

As with most fieldcraft decisions, this hide-and-seek contest becomes a waiting game. Hunkering under a tumbled Dabinett cider apple, I get as close to comfortable as possible; moulding my side into the contours of knotted bark, binoculars at the ready. *Your* move, mystery bird. Eventually a shadow appears and breaks cover. Flitting between apple twigs and mistletoe, it finally offers a clear view. A stunning orange breast contrasts against a glossy black beard. The matte grey cape that runs from the top of its head all the way down its back is scored with a striking splash of white eyeliner. This is a male redstart, in crisp breeding colours and recently arrived from Africa. He would have crossed the Dordogne a week ago and flown over sunseekers in the Costa del Sol a week before that. He's warning not *to* me, but *about* me. The *'tlack-tlack'* sound is alerting any potential females that there is danger nearby – and that *he* is excellent at keeping prospective wives safe from trouble. In reality, this is just a dress rehearsal, a matinee practice allowing him to flex his trills before the main event. Female redstarts always arrive a few days later, giving the boys a head start to case out and cherry-pick the best nest spots in time for their return.

Under the noisy bombardment of this new companion, I continue around Hop Kiln Orchard. While the apple and pear buds are still a month away from bursting, the orchard's hedgerows are stirring. Over a few days, the thorn-studded orchard perimeters transform as their ramparts are carpeted with a crisp white cloak of black-thorn blossom. Flowering well before their first leaves appear, this early pollen is vital for emerging insects, with each successful pollination initiating the development of a sloe berry. By summer, the nectar-producing shift has been largely taken over by meadow flowers, but in spring it is the boundary trees that ensure output is kept high on this essential production line.

The hedges around the orchards here are an eclectic mix of shapes and sizes, each bearing its own personality. Verdant and chaotic, they form a far cry from the skinny, flailed relics we've become accustomed to seeing in our ever more sanitised countryside. This wall of blackthorn stands over four metres tall and at least as many metres wide. It straddles the orchard on one side – and a humming wildflower meadow on the other. Yet just metres downstream, its character changes completely, giving way to a line of enormous old crack willows; the outgrown stalwarts of the Malverns' ancestral hedge-lines.

The ground underneath these feathered castles is littered with lost limbs. It's barely believable that some of these giant trees are still growing strong; huge cracks show where many were nearly torn open in past traumas. But these trees quickly heal from such scars. After all, they evolved alongside two of the greatest tree-fellers of them all: straight-tusked elephants and beavers. Despite being at opposite ends of the size spectrum, armed with brute strength, fine dentition and untiring persistence, these two species once felled enormous quantities of wood to feed insatiable appetites. In retaliation to these animal assaults, Europe's trees evolved many countermeasures. Everything from an elder's poisonous bark to the incredible growth spurts seen in willows, a lime's fortified buttress to the speed with which wild thorn trees mature, is an adaptation to counter the damage endured from rampant herbivory.

Today, with this landscape's elephants long gone, and beavers still a few years off returning joyously to this part of Herefordshire, the legacy of Britain's animal architects lives on in the extraordinary resilience of the orchard's willow hedge – and its striking ability to recover from the worst of wounds wrought by the British weather; a far lesser challenge than these billowing trees once faced prior to the dewilding of Britain.

Dividing Oak Orchard is an old, hard track; a short droving road that would have once provided the horse and its apple cart a highway to the old cider press. At some point in past history, a single row of hazels was planted along each side. Scarred with old coppice marks amid wrinkled bark, these are now some of the largest hazel trees we know; perhaps over a hundred years old.

Throughout the winter, these hazel trees play an unassuming role in the orchard – their nuts long foraged and their bare branches providing sustenance for only the hungriest herbivores. But in early spring, they wake from their dormant slumber and adorn our hedgerows, woodlands and coppices with a welcome sign that spring is imminent: catkins. These miniature lambs-tails always fascinated me as a child; their wriggling motion induced by the smallest of wobbles. Nature has a clever reason for their articulated bodies. Hazel trees are monoecious – meaning that both male and female flowers are found on the same tree. But each tree cannot pollinate itself. So, the catkins hang in the wind and with the lightest of breezes the fidgeting catkins release the tree's pollen into the air.

But this is only half the story. Catkins are the tree's male, pollen-producing flowers. But each hazel tree also produces tiny *female* flowers. These are far more exquisite, yet easily overlooked. Examined in the new year, the tree has what look like tiny demijohn-shaped buds, cushioned tightly next to finer branches. But as winter concedes to spring, these tiny champagne bottles pop to reveal a spout of wiry scarlet red petals. Just a few millimetres long, these female hazel flowers look like little sea anemones waving colourful tentacles: waiting to capture the windborne pollen.

Hazel has a clever adaptation to ensure its pollen carries as far as possible. Alongside the catkins emerging before the leaves to allow the pollen to travel further, each grain also repels others to keep it as light as possible. This anti-sticky property is ideal for reaching their target – binding with other pollen grains would weigh them down – but makes it hard for pollen-loving species such as bees to harvest. If bees collect too much, their pollen baskets simply empty en route back to the colony. In the regimented society of honeybees, they have learnt to collect just a little at a time – rather than risk returning empty handed.

As April blossoms, however, even the hazels will be upstaged. At the back of Maze Orchard, tucked among pollarded hazels, scrambling honeysuckle, clambering ivy and runaway pears, grow a handful of goat willows. Now, these inconspicuous trees, still devoid of any leaves, go through a remarkable transformation.

Shiny bubbles split open on their fine tapering branches,

revealing the tiny tips of furry catkins. Soon, the whole tree turns white, and then, pale green, as male catkins begin to advertise their pollen wares. As if from nowhere, hundreds of improbable flying machines – miniature black-and-yellow aircraft that even the finest physics and engineering minds have yet to replicate – arrive and converge on this ephemeral food source.

Finding ourselves below one of these trees on a calm and bright spring morning, Ben and I gawked in amazement as the air fizzed and the tree hummed with the sound of over-excited bees energetically working through the catkins. There was hardly a breeze in the air, yet a fine mist of pollen floated down, dislodged by a fervent whirlwind of hungry bees. For a generation raised in the silence of our chemical countryside, the noise generated by so many insects working overtime had to be heard to be believed: a *whole* tree engulfed by the whirring hum from a thousand tiny wings.

Just three generations ago, this buzzing bombardment would have been the norm in our hedgerows. Every wild cherry and damson, hawthorn and blackthorn, and each hazel and willow would have been smothered in bee sound as they blossomed. It's implausible to think that any of our grandparents, walking past such a spectacle, could have envisaged that this buzzing bombardment would become, within fifty years, a remarkable and noteworthy spectacle. Here in this little pocket of the Malverns, the landscape remains free from chemical input. The hedgerows are pollen-rich and as they fade, so the meadows take up the task of feeding the orchard's armies of bees. But this is the exception to the rule. Yeats's description of the countryside as 'bee-loud' is now largely an anachronism to our generation – and so each April we cherish the goat willow spectacle as much as we might the first sip of a new cider.

It is not only insects that thrive on the goat willow's bounty. In April each year, one of our most colourful garden visitors takes advantage of this glut. Blue tits spend a few busy weeks searching amid the hundreds of pinhead-sized flowers squeezed onto each willow catkin. It was once assumed that they were feeding on insects hiding among these small flowers, but the real reason is far more surprising. After many hours spent watching parties of blue tits foraging among willow catkins, it was proven that the birds specifically target the base of each catkin stalk. By pecking away at the nectaries found here, these sweet-toothed birds have learnt exactly how to extract this abundant nectar flow. It's easy to see why it didn't take blue tits long to learn that foil milk tops hid a sweet treat below.

But here the story takes a final twist. As blue tits sip on the willow's nectar, their pristine blue and white face masks become peppered with tiny pollen particles, turning the normally well-presented little birds into varying shades of mottled green and yellow. And as the blue tits move between catkins, looking hungrily for yet more nectar, these now panda-eyed passerines transfer pollen between different willow trees. This could well be the first example in Britain of a *bird* pollinating a tree.[1]

Once thought to be a club exclusively occupied by insects, it is now known that a few other animals across the world are capable of pollinating flowers. But these are normally creatures of jungle and cloud forest; the dazzling hummingbirds of the Americas or the giant fruit bats of the Indonesian jungle. Having our very own hummingbird proxy join the illustrious pollinator club shows that even our most common species still have their secrets to share.

For the whole of the winter, all of the orchard's slow worms have been deep underground. Unable to build a nest of their own to keep them from freezing, they have a method unique among British reptiles to stay warm while sleeping out the winter. If you can't produce much of your own body heat, it makes sense to steal it from another. As the temperature starts to cool in the autumn, slow worms seek out the entrances to meadow ant nests, exploiting any cracks in the parched summer soil to slither down into the master tunnel network. Here, these legless lizards find a chamber near the bottom of the ant nest, where they promptly curl up and fall asleep. The heat generated by the ant colony is enough to keep them from freezing, allowing them to hibernate from October to late March.

By early April, once the worst of the winter storms and chances of snow are long gone, the orchard's plentiful slow worms can be found sunning themselves – slowly reviving their weak metabolisms. It's always the youngsters that appear first – tiny stripy bootlaces, barely a forefinger's length. It's a wonder that these minuscule cold-blooded organisms are able to survive the winter at all. But like clockwork, each year they reappear – thanks to the warmth created by one of the orchard's most abundant yet often overlooked organisms: ants.

Within a week, the far larger adult slow worms will re-emerge – including chunky, pale-grey males, battle-scarred and stub-tailed. By the middle of the month, it's not uncommon to find a dozen curled up together; last year's youngsters dwarfed by the older generation they're intertwined with, as they share body heat absorbed from the warming spring sun.

Astonishingly, slow worms are among the longest living lizards in the world – regularly reaching thirty years of age,[2] with the oldest known specimen breaking half a century! They are also incredibly loyal to basking sites, so once you've found out their favoured tanning parlours, they can be easy to find on a warm morning. As they age, slow worms pick up distinctive scars from fights and predator escapes. I've now found one big old male here every year for the past five. Despite all these attributes, slow worms are the sorry owners of perhaps the least creative collective noun for our native fauna, having at some point been rather unoriginally assigned the grouping of 'a bunch'. It's high time these impressive creatures were afforded a better social designation – perhaps, a *spaghetti* of slow worms'.

Slow worms are not the only reptile to stir as the warmth of spring strikes the orchard soil. As the walls of the hop kiln heat up, a thriving colony of grass snakes, which are known to have called it home since at least the 1950s, sneak out to bask. Right below the cider mill, they move silently, nonchalantly, from beneath its loose bricks and into the open. Here, they lie – and wait. Not for prey, but for warmth. Having absorbed enough heat in this sheltered sun trap, they set off to scour the nearby pond for frogs. After a successful hunt, these adept swimmers return to land, silently reversing back into the safe confines of the hop-kiln walls. Like so much of the orchard's life, its grass snakes seamlessly blend into the human landscape.

New life isn't only being heard and seen in the orchard. April is the month that fires all of the senses, priming each with new sensations that remind us that spring is very much in the air. A short April shower has whipped up a cocktail of new smells, mixed with familiar ones arising from the damp meadow and drifting up through the fruit trees. Walking down to find the source uncovers a carpet of lush lime; the small stream running between the Maze and the Hop Kiln Orchards is now hidden between richly saturated leaves. The annual aroma of wild garlic, a pesto waiting to be plucked, has also returned. Crests of flawless star-shaped flowers adorn this low canopy, their crisp white offsetting the monotone of green below.

While it's rare to find bees tackling wild garlic flowers, they are used by one of our earliest-hatching butterfly species. Having overwintered as an inert pupae, a flash of orange gives away the location of a male orange-tip feeding among the white petals of wild garlic – his white underwing camouflaging well against the flowers he's drawing nectar from. Orange-tips appear throughout April, the males particularly unmistakable as they fly past with their namesake orange blotches adorning each wingtip. The conspicuous markings are thought to warn predators that these butter-flies are especially distasteful. They pick this up from the food they eat as caterpillars, accumulating the bitter compounds found in lady's smock and garlic mustard. It is these plants that our orange-tips are now searching for. The former prefers the dappled shade of hedgerows and wood-land margins; the latter thrives in damp grassland meadows. Every few years in the orchard there seems to be a bumper crop of lady's smock, as the small damp meadow between these orchards becomes awash with delicate flowers, their early growth-spurt pushing them above the grasses as they nod slowly in the breeze. Each flower-head has four iden-tical pale pink petals, which meet symmetrically at their pale green centre. From this pungent crop carries the scent that draws the orange-tip in to lay its eggs.

The female orange-tip won't, however, settle for any flower; she is an exceedingly discerning customer when it comes to deciding where to deposit her eggs. If the flower-head won't support her weight, she rejects it. If the inflorescence is too small, she rejects it. If it is too old, she rejects it. Working through the meadow like Goldilocks tasting porridge, she looks for a large flower that is just opening, on a strong stem. Having found one that is just right, she carefully lays *one* egg. Never more. Her egg is coated in a pheromone that tells other female orange-tips that *her* egg was here first. She will fly for days repeating this process many times, carefully seeking out new flowers that haven't yet been laid on, always laying just one egg – then moving on. The female orange-tip has good reason to be so careful. Her larvae, if given the chance, very much live up to the *Hungry Caterpillar* idiom. Infant orange-tips are cannibals. If a small caterpillar, its egg laid later, hatches next to a larger cousin – it will be lunch time. So, by meticulously checking each flower for eggs or pheromones before they lay, female orange-tips prevent their next generation from becoming lunch for a caterpillar which has hatched from a previously laid egg. Allowing their progeny to dine alone ensures that each year, we get to enjoy these stunning little butterflies flitting through this meadow.

In the natural world, there are species whose actions go far beyond the food chains within which they sit. They are known as ecosystem engineers – animals that, just by *being*, enrich their environment exponentially. Beavers are a famous example. By coppicing their food trees, they promote dense shrubby growth; essential feeding sites for dozens of moth species which in turn generate rich hunting opportunities for bats. Their dams – an innate response to the sound of flowing water – create pools of calm water, vital nursery grounds for fish and amphibians. The riffles generated down-stream of these timber blockades create a faster-flowing spawning habitat for salmonids. Just by *doing what they do*, as they chew and swim and shuffle about their daily lives, beavers fill the world around them with diverse life.

In the orchard, there are three equally important species – ones that create the means for others to thrive here in this crowded jungle. Our three native woodpeckers act as the canopy's ecosystem engineers: the flying beavers of the treetops. Their habit of scouring away at loose bark and digging out invertebrates creates new feeding sites for fungal spores – in turn generating more deadwood. The prolific cavity-creation of woodpeckers also ensures a steady supply of new nesting sites for the orchard's other birds, mammals and insects. Woodpeckers are nature's carpenters: highly-skilled workers with a toolkit that allows them to chisel out the finest real estate. Each pair can produce up to half a dozen completed and semi-completed nest holes each season; from the diminutive fifty-pence piece entrances made by lesser spotted woodpeckers – the perfect home for a blue tit – to the doughnut-sized openings of green woodpeckers – the ideal dark chimney nest site for a jackdaw.

The orchard property market is now a thriving business. Each year, new species join the growing list of those who have owned a woodpecker home. Working between the different orchard trees on a mid-month nest survey, making notes of which favoured cavities had their usual occupiers – either jackdaws, tits or redstarts – in residence, we aligned the ladders on the crumbling fork of an old Yarlington Mill. Propped next to two large dead stumps generously left in situ by Nancy and David, trekking up the ladders unveiled a partially excavated green woodpecker nest hole.

With no sign of life at the entrance, I pushed back a piece of mistletoe that had grown across it, fired up the light on my endoscope, and used it to peer in. The occupants weren't too fond of this plan, for as soon as an image appeared on the monitor, I nearly fell off the ladder as three fire-coloured heads shot upwards. Less than twenty-four hours old, the eyes of these robin chicks were still glued firmly shut; over-sized dark orbs hidden behind a fine layer of tissue-thin skin. The rustling of my approach had induced a feeding response, as three vivid pink necks strained to the limit in the hope of receiving a fresh caterpillar. Their wide mouths, the perimeter lined with bright yellow, showed off a bright orange gape – an unmistakable landing site for a parent returning with a tasty morsel for their brood hidden in this dark hollow. Unlike blue tit chicks, born completely bald, these robin chicks were covered with the finest down feathers. Running up from their backs, and capped off with little afros, the three chicks nestled together, efficiently displaying a fine carpet of down acting as a blanket to keep their three tiny bodies warm. Knowing how territorial robins can be, it was time to hastily retreat – just in time to hear the familiar ticking-off from the nearby bushes, as one of the parents scolded our presence. Finding a robin – a hugely secretive and territorial nester – in an exposed cavity three metres up in an orchard tree proves just how much compe-tition there is for nest sites here, and how important the continued presence of woodpeckers is for our woodland creatures.

Everything from grey squirrels to hornets, tawny owls to hazel dormice and even stoats and common toads line up to take advantage of the nesting and roosting sites created by the orchard's cabinet-makers. But for many, finding the right home in our ever-fracturing countryside is becoming harder every year. Marsh tits, for example, have been seen to steal the nests of lesser spotted woodpeckers.[3] While both still live here in the orchard, such interactions have vanished from most British woodlands. And with tree homes in such short supply, and standing dead trees increasingly rare, some species have had to innovate.

A walk around the orchards towards the end of April turns up one such character. On a second pass of the day through Hop Kiln Orchard's large jackdaw colony – a group of veteran trees riddled with cavities – Ben and I are stopped dead in our tracks. There, nestled up on a branch, in broad daylight, is a young and incredibly fluffy baby tawny owl. We had already walked past this same tree earlier, apparently oblivious to the fact that a young owlet was likely eyeballing us the whole time. The youngster, as with most daytime owls, is remarkably relaxed in the presence of people, keeping one eye on us while the other does its best to appear asleep. This is a bird that is supposed to relish the peace and quiet of a dark, tangled woodland. Yet here it sat – surrounded by the sprawling high-rise of jackdaw apartments; a hermit voluntarily taking up residence in Trafalgar Square.

Tentatively peering into the nearest jackdaw hole revealed that this cavity had been commandeered. Tawny owls are Britain's most successful owl species, and this was just another reminder of why. While the jackdaws were more than happy to take on a buzzard here, they had most likely learnt to steer well clear of taking on their fluffy neighbour, for fear perhaps of being struck in their sleep by its fierce nocturnal parents.

Surprisingly, considering the active tawny nest at their centre, the adjacent jackdaw city was thriving, its first chicks having hatched in the past few days. Now, nestled among cradles of sheep's wool and dried grasses, each contained a small huddle of completely bald, salmon-pink hatchlings. At this age, their necks look extraordinarily long, inter-twined as the sleeping newborns wait for their next feed. The arrival of these ugly ducklings – a far cry from the glossy-capped adult jackdaws in their edgy grey suits – is a key turning point in the orchard calendar.

Towards the end of the month, the first wave of big orchard beetles arrives. Cockchafers – unmistakably huge night-fliers – begin to stir, up to a metre below the soil. Having spent up to four years as larvae, feeding on tubers and roots before pupating, they hatch deep underground and then crawl upwards to emerge from subterranean sanctums. Despite all of this effort, the adult beetle lives topside for only a few weeks, spending just 3 per cent of its life on the wing. This probably accounts for the cockchafer's dreadful aerobatics, as it's common to find them bumbling their way into windows, doors and even people for this brief period – appar-ently blindly flying about on the search for food and a mate. Cockchafers are often drawn into moth traps too, creating a good opportunity to tell the difference between sexes when holding them side-by-side. The boys are adorned with oversized feathery plumes on each antenna – used to help them detect the pheromone trails left by females in the night air – while their counterparts have petite little plumes.

The history of the cockchafer is fascinating. Once a hugely populous British species, in the early twentieth century, millions of freshly emerged beetles could be found in a few square miles of woodland. But their fate took a sharp dip after the Second World War, as intensive and indiscriminate pesticide use hit them at every stage of their lifecycle. Prior to the invention of pesticides, cockchafers were considered serious pests. They once reached such numbers in Avignon during the Middle Ages that some of the insects were brought to court and ordered to withdraw within three days. Unsurprisingly, the insects failed to comply with their sentence, and the locals were ordered to collect and kill every last cockchafer they could find.[4] More locally, in 1574, so many cockchafers hatched in the Severn Valley that their carcasses, drifting downstream, clogged up and disabled watermills.[5]

Today nothing approaching these numbers is seen, as the species continues trying to recover from its near eradication, but it's still a joy to find them flying around as spring reaches its peak. Here in the orchard, bordered by woodland and meadow, the mature oak trees coming into bud provide the adult beetles with their main leaf diet for their short lives. But beyond their bumbling and carefree characters, these bugs play a vital role in the orchard restaurant as they crash around the trees each April.

Now is the time that most of the orchard's bats will emerge. One – our largest – thrives in the woodpecker-generated network of treetop cavities. After awakening from hibernation, a female noctule bat will fertilise her single egg with sperm, stored from mating the previous summer. She will have spent up to six months asleep, living purely off her fat reserves – so awakes very, very hungry. Large beetles and the first of the macro moths to hatch are exactly what she needs, spending every suitable evening out hunting for them. Noctules are usually the first species to emerge each evening, allowing us up to an hour at sunset to watch them in the dying light as they expertly home in on their noisy cockchafer targets. Watching these large bats clatter into their large prey, embracing them with a nimble scoop of their tails, which guides the unfortunate beetle up towards their wide and tooth-studded gape, it seems hard to believe we are sitting in a farmed landscape of twenty-first-century Britain.

Now, one of the orchard's most important animals is stirring. She, too, will rely on the action of predators if she is to make her summer's home. After a winter spent underground living off their meagre fat reserves, giant bumblebee queens emerge on the point of starvation.

Having hibernated up to nine months, finding early nectar and pollen is vital. Without pollen, a queen bee's ovaries won't develop, leaving her unable to start a colony. Those that make it to our goat willows stock up on their pollen bounty – then set out on a very specific mission.

Walking among the orchard glades at this time of year, it's not uncommon to jump slightly. A deep drone resonates around your ankles, as if a tiny lawnmower has started working away at your shoelaces. Looking down reveals a large bumblebee queen, flying slowly and intently past, sweeping close to the ground. Her sluggish speed might imply laziness, but in fact she is working incredibly hard;

every one of her senses deliberately primed to detect the faintest scent in the vegetation. Our queen is looking for somewhere to nest. For that, she first needs to detect a most specific scent: rodent wee.

The reason is simple. Old mouse and vole nests are the ideal place for the bumble queen to raise her enormous family. A tunnel of just the right width and length is already bored into the ground, leading to a moss-lined chamber of just the right volume. As soon as she detects the right scent, the queen locks onto the trail through the foliage; a tiny chinook carefully manoeuvring through the perils of low-altitude flight. Her eyes scan as she flies – looking for the two-pence-piece-sized entrance hole of her new home. Queen bees must have some way of telling that a rodent nest is no longer occupied, because startling a dozing mouse could land her in serious trouble. But if crawling along a dark tunnel *doesn't* result in a face full of whiskers, then there's a good chance that the queen has found exactly what she's looking for: a vacant moss- and hay-lined apartment to adopt as her own.

Like all new home-owners, she soon sets to work adding her own touches to the place. Many trips up and down her tunnel are made to remove unwanted items left by the previous occupants. Fetid stockpiles of grain are expelled with the fervour of someone replacing an avocado bathroom suite. Anything too heavy to lift is coated in her antibacterial wax, removing the risk of bacteria or fungi attacking the precious eggs she is waiting to lay. With her fastidious spring-cleaning complete, the queen bumble starts the conversion. Her single-room apartment is soon going to become a particularly bespoke nursery.

Using thin wax sheets exuded from between the segments of her abdomen, the queen fashions two miniature cups. The first she fills with honey; a selectively distilled soup of nectar and digestive enzymes. This forms a backup larder, should the weather turn and leave her unable to forage. Adjacent to this honeypot, her second wax cup is filled with pollen. This is the cradle for her infants yet to be. As the tits in the apple trunks above get down to laying eggs in their mossy homes, so, below the roots of the orchard, Queen Bumbles does the same. She lays a dozen white eggs, crawls on top of her little nest, and settles down to incubate her eggs. For four days, the devoted mother keeps her developing brood warm using her own body heat.

As soon as the bumble brood hatch, the mother's work is really cut out. Young bumblebee larvae have voracious appetites – growing fast on a diet of pollen. The queen can visit up to six thousand flowers a day, juggling foraging with incubating – ensuring that her larvae always remain well-fed, while also ensuring the colony doesn't lose the heat that is critical for successful development. But all this work is well worth the effort, for once this first brood of teenage bees finally fledges, the queen has a dozen new workers to help the colony thrive.

Now, instead of foraging, the queen can switch to full-time egg-laying. With each new generation, this little factory ramps up its output; churning out worker bees that rush around the orchard, pollinating every flower they can find. In just a few weeks, large colonies can grow to as many as 350 workers. And this is the secret to the success of a healthy orchard.

Apple and pear flowers are almost exclusively pollinated

by bees. Here in Britain, we have over 250 different species of social and solitary bee – and a large percentage of these can be found in our traditional orchards. Were bees to vanish from the orchard, as they are from surrounding orchards due to the systemic use of pesticides, then the entire ecosystem of the orchard, its financial output and its autumn cider, would all collapse. Bees, social or solitary, are integral to the interlinked food webs of this fruiting forest. But so too are all the other players in the orchard's complex game.

Without the winter fruits and hazelnuts, there would be no food source to see our skipping mice or shuffling voles through the winter. Without the orchard's thriving tawny owls, few other hunters would ensure such a steady supply of vacant rodent burrows; a bankable housing market for the orchard's bumblebees. And without spring pollinators such as bumblebees, the pollination of the very orchard itself would cease. Natural regulation is what makes the orchard flourish – and what renders it as much a natural ecosystem as a farmed environment. We remove any one of its players at our peril.

MAY

HOME, SWEET HOME

BEN

In the month of May when all leaves open,
I see when I walk how well all things
Lean on each other.

ROBERT BLY

May is the month when you would be mad to be anywhere but home. One year, I was weathering the harsh Mongolian steppes, filming wild horses, when Nick sent me a photo. It showed a redstart, a flash of borrowed orange on extended holiday from Africa. It was frozen in motion, alighting at the edge of a gnarled Thorn pear where it had hidden its nest; a sagging old tree I had walked past many times before. Behind it fuzzed a sea of silver blossom. And at that moment, even the bleak purple steppes, infinitely wilder and less populated than anywhere in Britain, were no replacement for the call of May back home.

May is the fizzing month, the bursting month, the blossom-frothing month. It is the month of improbable change that you somehow never see coming, even though your mind knows to expect it every year. No matter how many Mays you live through, or will ever live through, the surprise of the seasons is perhaps more pronounced on our little Atlantic island than anywhere on Earth. Surprise you it will – and always does.

May is the time, the moment, when Britain regains its three-dimensional verdure. Deep trees burst towards you with emerald added, as if you've just put on 3-D glasses in a cinema – or watched dreary wartime footage gain the colour that suddenly grabs your emotions. Oaks bubble with resurgent leaves. Their crunched, dead skeletons transform into chlorophyll cathedrals. The lurid greens are intense and, at first, unreal.

New melodies ambush the rusty listener, who hasn't heard them in eight long months. The dense blackthorns develop a mechanical, sewing-machine chatter: the lesser whitethroat is back in its favourite hedge. The goat willows, growing fuzzier by the day, hear the clear descant of the willow warbler. The densest, bushiest of hedgerows will, some days later, hear the speeded-up-blackbird song of the garden warbler; a rasping chaos of fluid notes. One day, these bushes lie quiet and unadorned. The next, as if someone has flicked a studio switch, a new layer of the orchestra fades up – fresh from the African winter. Soon, all around the orchard, little kingdoms of thorns, willows and the nooks of old fruit trees are defended with melodic ferocity. One song carries from the willows – tied to no one, no place: 'Cuck-oo'.

Life here has now very much awoken, and the fruit trees – on the edge of popping into blossom – begin to come alive with the sights, sounds and smells of a vibrant community of beings all courting, building and hatching. This is the start of the orchard's most productive month. Tucked away from view, under leaves, deep in cavities and even underground, organisms are growing fast. While the first chicks, caterpillars and young mammals remain vulnerable and secretive for now, most of this life will soon burst free. All creatures here have put on a turn of speed, as the first song thrushes fledge below hatchling swallows, bees work overtime to collect pollen, and hundreds of bats hawk among the apples and pears each night. May is the month to spend as much time as possible immersing oneself in the orchard's song – and each visit will turn up something new.

Life bursts. But how does it know to burst at all? Many of us take it for granted that most of our trees shed their leaves in winter, then wake up and rapidly don thick coats in time for summer. Many orchard growers know that should you cut an apple branch in March and bring it inside, it will flower in a water-filled vase within a matter of weeks. Bring in the same branch in November, and it will not. But why?

To give us the May spectacle they do, Britain's trees have been quietly preparing for months. The autumn before, trees sense the growing length of the winter night via the medium of phytochrome, a molecule that is extremely receptive to red light. In the absence of sufficient volumes of red-wave sunlight, the phytochrome 'deactivates' – returning to its inert, native state. During the growing cold and dark of late autumn and winter, no longer fuelled by lengthy periods of daylight, the long periods of dark excite the tree's production of abscisic acid. This acid inhibits the growth of new buds, hardening the tree, as its vibrant, pulsing tissues transform into a fortress of cold timber – capable of resisting the extremes of winter.

By December, even unseasonable spells of warmth do little to stir our trees from their skeletal slumber. Not unlike the many insects and amphibians that survive the orchard's winter, our willows, oaks and apples, too, begin to evacuate water from their cells. The latest research suggests that a number of genes remain active in our trees even during periods of the deepest sleep. These genes act in particular to protect vital cells inside the tree from the stress of dehydration, as the trees effectively drain large parts of themselves of the waters used for growth. In the cruel months of January and February, however, this gene activity is hampered by the cold. So to add further protection to the cells during their slumber, trees convert starches within their sleeping limbs into a sugar-rich antifreeze. This allows the trees to keep water cool, but not freezing, within their boughs – thereby keeping vital tissues intact during the harshest of months.

During this largely dormant phase, when our trees undergo regular temperatures of around six degrees Celsius, they begin to accumulate what scientists call 'chill hours'.

Though not yet fully defined, it appears that trees are capable of registering, numbering, the cold hours they are exposed to across a season's course; generally, those falling below six degrees. Intriguingly, when the temperature falls below minus one degree Celsius, however, the trees stop 'counting' at all. As winter progresses, these 'chill hours' accumulate. And to be sensitive to the wake-up calls of spring, with its lengthening days and warming sunlight, a certain number of 'chill hours', those falling between zero and six degrees, must first accrue. As the trees' winter slumber progresses, however, other genes within their boughs begin to stir. These awaking genes encourage production of vitamin C and antioxidants. These are thought to help rid the tree of oxidants that would damage plant tissue, if still around when the tree begins to grow come the spring.

Even now, the science of a tree's winter life cycle is neither perfect nor complete. Standing silently beside us every day, even the most basic mysteries of trees have yet to be fully resolved, nor is every secret hidden in their boughs likely to be laid bare for many years to come.

As the spring arrives, the weather, as a rule, gets warmer. In truth, however, it is not so much the pulse of warmth but the dwindling duration of dark hours which triggers our trees' longer-term response to 'wake up'. Come late March, the lengthening periods of sunlight kick-start new molecular pathways. Phytochrome, in the words of American horticulturalist Scott Aker, acts as 'a seasonal hourglass'.[1] As the dark hours of spring decrease, our trees are induced by their invisible molecular component, light-sensitive phytochrome, to awaken. At the same time, the growing warmth is what induces our trees to begin opening their buds.[2]

In our ever less predictable springs, as the climate changes and seasonal chaos becomes an ever more regular event, even trees can be deceived. On occasion, they unfold their leaves too early – only for brutal frosts to strike them a few weeks later. In most seasons, however, our adopted orchard still pulses with a regular riot of greens come early May.

As the larger trees uncurl after the winter, the orchard's protective fortress walls of blackthorn are by now verdant, impenetrable and heaving with life. Few butterflies pass by without stopping – and a steady procession of holly blues, speckled woods and brimstones, together with ever-emerging numbers of peacocks, red admirals and small tortoiseshells, flicker through its thorny reaches. The apartment block inside a blackthorn bush is hard to penetrate without serious damage to my remaining hair – but on easing its spikes apart with a thick hazel stick, I will often discover punky broods of song thrushes wedged into their mud-lined nests. With a ladder – and still greater discomfort – you can find the scruffy, webby nests of bullfinches near the very top. Yet while blackthorn is a vital resource in late April and early May, many of the orchard's birds have been waiting for an even more important event. It would once have kicked spring life into action across almost 60 per cent of our island's landmass. The oak leaves begin to open. And for one of this orchard's most special birds, their chicks will hatch as the oak leaves burst.

A fraction larger than a blue tit, lesser spotted woodpeckers spend most of their lives in complete silence, many metres above your head. It is one of the few birds to spend a significant portion of its life upside-down, where its dappled black and white zebra-markings blend, perfectly, with the play of light and shade in the very highest limbs of the alders, willows and birches. But its lifeblood remains the insects it will uncover in the unfolding oak leaves of late spring.

By March and early April, lesser spotted woodpeckers move from far-ranging forays through the tall, rotting trees where they seem to spend much of their time in winter, and begin, on rare occasions, to show some interest in one another. It's in these fleeting moments that you can catch the pair broadcasting, for all of thirty seconds, where they are. The same drumming trees are remembered year on year. The dead Hop Kiln Orchard oak is where we sit and wait each spring – and it is from here that the drumming of these birds tells us they have survived another harsh Malverns winter.

Their whole lives based around secrecy and evasion, lesser spotted woodpeckers do not court where they make their home. After a remarkable treetop display, where the male dances like a butterfly around the female on his dappled, rounded wings, the pair will suddenly depart and bounce away into the distance, as we furiously scramble to follow them back to their nest tree of choice. Here, crumbling white poplars, ragged white willows, the dead limb of an oak or the lifeless snag of a living apple can all be made home by lesser spotted woodpeckers. It seems like a needle in a haystack – but every bird has certain 'tells'. Nick and I know almost every potential nesting tree by the names we have plotted on a map. Meticulously, quietly working through the trees, we tick them off as we go. We do not pause beside living trees or young ones, but instead, scour every decaying stump or snag with our straining eyes.

For three years, the woodpeckers have chosen to nest in apple trees. For two years, the soft, dead snag of a live tree provided their chosen home, but in one, the canny birds nested within a thriving jackdaw colony, drilling into the trunk of a decaying Strawberry Norman. The nest was successful, and we wondered whether the jackdaws didn't keep potential nest predators away. When nesting away from the orchard, lesser spotted woodpecker nests can be fiendishly hard to detect. I have found holes drilled into the dead snags of poplars, more than thirty metres above the ground. Nests in fungal alders are drilled into the shady, sloping underside of trees, where deep shadows make them very hard to see.

As if finding a nest the size of a fifty-pence piece within the orchard maze doesn't challenge us enough, these tiny woodpeckers will visit a number of properties before committing to their summer home. Architecturally curious, they excavate nests and then give up. Infuriatingly, they also build second homes alongside their first, and excavate multiple nests at the same time. Often, first attempts will be taken over by their great-spotted cousins, so lesser spotted woodpeckers have developed the sensible idea of keeping a second or even third home on stand-by. On occasions, woodpeckers of all species simply make mistakes.

They start drilling and then, like a builder hitting concrete instead of the expected brickwork, back off and reconsider. But sometimes, you get lucky.

In 2015, I passed the old Kingston Black in the very middle of May. A faint begging call was coming from within – and there, rounded to factory-level perfection, was a fifty-pence-sized nest hole, drilled into a dead snag of the veteran tree. Scarcely hoping, I drew back – and then in bounced a male lesser spotted woodpecker. A study in red, white and black, he reversed down the tree like a clockwork toy, before vanishing through his perfectly circular front door. The chicks were still small – and for days to come, we would study them with all the care and attention of someone watching the last living specimens of its species.

As we began our photographic study, using a carefully-placed remote camera to photograph the prey items coming to the nest, the woodpeckers were transformed – from elusive enigmas to trusting companions. Within two days, the male was happily alighting on top of Nick's camera; finding it a useful place to assemble the caterpillars in his bill before flitting to the nest hole and diving in.

Now, we could watch every flight and foray – to every tree. The outgrown willows proved to be the male's favourite larder. On dozens of occasions, he would bound to their furry crown, clambering around upside-down, digging juicy beetle larvae from just under the surface of its finest branches. His work was never random. He would tap then listen. Then he would rip out a wiggling grub and bound back towards the nest. His wife, however, did not agree with his choice of restaurant. She favoured the crowns of the Hop Kiln Orchard oaks. Three hundred years old, they provided her with an ever-growing bounty of caterpillars. Each day, tension came as the lesser spot's main predator, the great spotted woodpecker, came ever closer to the nest. The wary parents would hide, calling from a distance. As the chicks grew ever louder, we feared more and more that this zealous summer carnivore would dig them from their nests. But then, one day, the nest was silent. Close-by, three downy woodpecker chicks were found, being contentedly fed in the crown of an apple. The extraordinary efforts of the parents had paid off.

Not every year would be like this one. The next spring, Nick found the pair in the dead branches of an old Yarlington Mill. The spring seemed idyllic, but the caterpillar crop was poor. In place of caterpillars, in came a less nourishing flow of bark lice, gleaned from the apple trees – a measly brunch compared to the rich steak provided by oak moth caterpillars.

For lesser spotted woodpeckers to survive in the long term, studies have shown that pairs should fledge at least three chicks, ideally four or five. For this to happen, the bounty of deadwood-snatched insects brought to the nest must be continuous and calorific. Like so many species in the orchard, lesser spotted woodpeckers have built their life cycles around the bounty provided by ancient trees. In this orchard, the menu is still rich. The alder swamp provides cranefly larvae. The apples crawl with the larvae of beetles and flies. But it is the time-battered willows and oaks, in their unbroken lines, which most often prove the salvation of these vanishing birds.

Our adopted orchard, we believe, sits within a line of ancient trees and copses that forms the greatest unnoticed, continuous woodland in our country. Vast reserves of old willow, perhaps the largest in Britain, still line streamsides in a county where a historic lack of arable farming has preserved the outgrown hedge-lines of two centuries ago. Enormous stands of veteran oak can still be found across this landscape. We have calculated that even today, you could cross Herefordshire, from the south to the north, without departing from a line of old willows or oaks.

In our view, far stronger protective statutes should be placed on the immense line of mature deciduous trees that runs largely unbroken from Greater Malvern all the way north to the Wyre Forest. Here lies a vast corridor of woodland that, with sufficient vision, could be protected, and expanded, in the decades to come. While rewilding can, in a small space of time, transform the ground layer into something wonderful and diverse, it takes hundreds of years for willows and oaks to reach their finished forms. Once gone, they are gone for centuries to come. So the 'Malvern Corridor', as we term it, may yet prove to be one of the most valuable of all refuges for the giant wood pasture trees that once dominated the whole of the British Isles – and for one of our least seen yet most important species.

What studying lesser spotted woodpeckers has shown us is how certain species act as invaluable indicators of the health of our countryside – and the changes within it. Through their tiny life dramas, we have learned about what happens in bad summers; about the importance of old trees

– and the crucial importance of standing deadwood across large areas of land. These traditional orchards act as nature's Petri dishes, in which the wins and woes of the wider landscape play out.

Many of the May journeys we witness are small ones. The wood mice creeping through the boughs in search of food. The nesting birds making forays to feed their chicks. The goshawks flashing through the apples, on the hunt for unwary pheasants or woodpigeons. But May is also the time when far greater journeys finally come to an end. Of all our visitors, no voyage is more amazing than that under-taken by another of our orchard favourites: the spotted flycatcher.

Theirs is a journey that begins in the warmth of the Gambian winter, though some British birds are believed to fly as far south as the Congo. It is good that birds are not known to suffer from culture shock in the way some humans do, because in the course of just a couple of months, spotted flycatchers will move from humid forests through Bedouin dunes to the bucolic orchards of the Malverns. They will commence their journey with forest primates, bridge it with camels – and end it with horses and sheep.

On just one occasion, I have intercepted these remark-able birds en route, as I sat by an oasis in the Erg Chebbi dunes of Morocco – and watched flycatchers fall out of the sky. As I looked on, nightingales, warblers and shrikes all tumbled out of the scorching blue and into the cooler green of the tamarisks. Here the flycatchers were arriving to take water, insects and rest beside many other more exotic species: woodchats heading to the Mediterranean, and a fierce, confused Scops owl perhaps headed to some crumbling old village in southern France.

It's rare to see familiar British birds at the very nadir of their migration; at the time most likely to kill them. You gain respect for their endeavours as you watch these tiny birds brave the Saharan sunshine, determined to reach our gardens and orchards each summer. After crossing the Sahara, many of our spotted flycatchers take a westerly route through the Iberian Peninsula. They then work their way northwards before crossing the Channel to join us. One spotted flycatcher – flying from a moist forest in the Gambia to the pastoral environs of the Malverns – makes a journey of around 4,800 kilometres (2,980 miles) to reach the hop-kiln walls. When they do arrive, many spotted flycatchers return to *exactly* where they were raised.

In spite of the extraordinary distance of the spotted flycatcher's annual migration to this orchard, the precision with which one female in particular finds her home has never ceased to amaze us. In the missing brick of the hop kiln, just a foot above the ground, she has, in all but one year, placed her nest: an atomic space compared to the vastness of her journey. Selecting nest sites within days of arrival, our flycatchers then get down to the serious business of skewering anything unlucky enough to fly past their killing trees of choice.

Of the hapless butterflies we see crammed into their bills,

speckled woods and ringlets are often high on the menu. Hornets have been watched being unceremoniously thrashed against the top of the telegraph post. Honeybees, bumble-bees, solitary bees, wasps, bee-flies, wasp impersonators and a huge array of hoverflies are caught in stunningly fast sallies from the tops of the Hop Kiln Orchard trees. One pear near the gate appears to provide the perfect airspace for aerial annihilation. Perhaps more insects have died suddenly passing this one spot than most other areas in our country-side as yet untouched by pesticides.

Often, up to three pairs of flycatchers have haunted the hop-kiln and farmhouse buildings alone. In exceptional years, as many as six pairs have wedged their nests in its maze of ivy, clematis, wisteria and missing bricks – and fierce competition over the pear-tree kill zone has broken out. In this orchard, and its wider environs of oak-edged horse fields, we found as many as twenty breeding pairs in 2015; the one year we were able to survey every tree. This is a number of spotted flycatchers larger than that now found in some counties – contained in an area of 800 by 600 *metres*. We cherish our spotted flycatchers as the most invaluable of all canaries in the ecological goldmine of the orchard. At the moment, their bee-catching success is all the more staggering when set against the picture of national decline. Since 1970, spotted flycatchers have declined by 87 per cent, yet even these statistics mask a longer trend: we lost half of our birds before this, between 1955 and 1965 alone. A century before, they were deemed among the commonest of all England's summer visitors.[3]

The living expression of aerial insect abundance, the

flycatcher's decline has not occurred across the board. The vast, unsprayed areas that constitute much of northern and western Scotland have not seen these birds vanish. Nor has the large food-rich New Forest, where the *'zick'* call of the flycatcher, like a begging chick, remains a common sound. At a more local level, some large, garden-rich, bee-rich areas of Worcestershire and Herefordshire have remained a valuable stronghold for spotted flycatchers. In contrast, in areas dominated by arable farmland and chemical use, such as the East Anglian counties, spotted flycatchers have become endangered refugees; the birds of large villages[4] where the worst effects of flying insect removal have yet to take place. Each year, we cherish not only our flycatchers' extraordinary journey – but the fact we still have them at all.

Usually, by the last day in May, our spotted flycatchers can be detected, their silvery chins and beady black eyes watching us from carefully concealed nests, as they complete their clutch of four to five marbled eggs. Two weeks later, these will hatch – and the life of the orchard's butterflies and bees becomes progressively more miserable. Invariably, flycatchers like to see over the top of their nests; perhaps to spot their orchard nemesis, nest-raiding jays, in time to evacuate. Each year, 'stupid' nests – generally those we find the quickest – are also first to be spotted by jays. Canny nests, deep in mistletoe, ivy or old woodpecker holes, stand a far better chance of success. After several years of staring assiduously at lines of crawling wisteria, we know where to spot the nests of flycatchers on the hop kiln – and their ancestral use of nest sites makes our life easier. We'll spend hours at a time watching, often using the car as a hide, to see what twitching victims are brought in. But in some years, the surrounding landscape deals our flycatchers a horrible surprise.

Half a kilometre away, Nancy's neighbours manage their orchard very differently to ours. Every week, sometimes every day, vast quantities of chemicals are sprayed onto their orchard – and the apples that we eat. And as we watch the bees returning to their orchard hives, you see first hand the devastating effect of indiscriminate pesticide use. Some bees appear visibly confused and disoriented. Others die in front of our eyes – you can, on occasions, watch bees dropping from the air and twitching pathetically on the ground, their tracheal tubes stuffed full of toxins. In the last two seasons, we have noticed a dramatic decline in the overall number of honeybees on the wing. And last year, that decline made its inevitable presence felt – as only half of our flycatchers appeared to be showing signs of successfully nesting at all. In spite of the fact that the orchard's apples, poplars, willows, oaks, thorn hedges and flower-filled gardens pump out a mass of flying invertebrate targets each summer, it can be easy to forget that this orchard is a hostage to the wider landscape, too.

Since many populations of flycatchers in our villages now number just single pairs, it is sadly inevitable that we will soon start seeing them vanish from the map entirely, as these island populations prove too small to survive. But the apparently small-scale successes of this orchard, and its gardens, may soon prove far more important than we might imagine. These nectar-rich landscapes may decide whether the spotted flycatcher can still be watched hunting in our country a century from now.

The orchard provides a sharing arrangement that shows farmland can still work in tandem with our vanishing insectivores. Ironically, the very parasites and larvae that the neighbouring orchards spray against, at huge economic cost, are removed free of charge here by the orchard's biomass of very hungry birds. Many wood- or fruit-boring species, damaging to commercial apple trees, are expertly killed not by costly chemicals – but flycatchers, for free. Like barn owls in a farmer's outbuilding, flycatchers might be seen as England's most delightful pest-removal service. But as they transform into aerial torpedoes each May, we never take them for granted. Unless we can find ways to keep the airways around our adopted orchard alive, their time, too, is running out.

Another success story in the orchard, with its large areas of open ground and hollow Thorn pears, is that of the redstart. In most years, this orchard holds five pairs – attesting, this time, to the abundance of food that this wood-pasture specialist finds on the ground. From mid-April, the males have been blasting away their rattle from the tops of the cherries. Then, in the second week of May, silence falls. The redstarts vanish. It is at this time that the female is sitting tucked away on up to eight azure-blue eggs – in a nest generally lined with sheep's wool and, most often, a few pieces of string. Female redstarts are fussy nesters. The opposite of the flycatchers, they delve deep into the hollow heart of fruit trees. The darker and more twisting the tree cavity, the more chances it has a redstart tucked deep inside. Fortunately for the purposes of study, redstarts can also be fooled. In 2012, I began to design nest boxes based on the advice of naturalist Douglas Miller. Doug had realised that redstarts love to tuck themselves around a corner, and so designed a box with a hollow entrance on the left, a baffle with a hole at the back, and a very dark space on the right where the redstart can nest as she prefers – in near total darkness. Within the first year, these boxes worked a treat. It is always satisfying to see birds return each year from Africa – but moving straight into your lovingly-crafted furniture, tied to a tree, even more so. These nest boxes have allowed us to study how redstarts are using the orchard – and thriving.

In the last few days of May, our redstarts hatch, and suddenly you can see the wary males again, uttering their angry 'shweep' call as you venture too close to their crumbling pear tree cathedrals. Orchards, if unsprayed, and their old trees left, are actually a prime habitat for redstarts. These open wood pastures afford them cavities in which to nest, but grazed, open grounds on which to feed. The density in this orchard is far higher than anywhere I have been except the New Forest – and much higher than the gloomy, darker woods of our near neighbour, the Forest of Dean. Due to the current geographical range limitations of the redstart, those people living in Herefordshire and Worcestershire will be those most able to help and protect orchard redstarts in the years to come. Leaving old pears, in particular, seems to benefit them, as the cavities often run deeper than apple. In 2018, for the first time, we found redstarts nesting in old green woodpecker holes in an old pear; a breed rather memorably named the Stinking Bishop – another lovely example of orchard 'recycling'.

But we have also searched dozens of sprayed orchards in the surrounding land for redstarts too – and didn't find a single one. Here crawl few beetles, leatherjackets or other invertebrates to be snatched on red tail-flashing forays onto green pasture. For orchards to harbour redstarts, starlings and many other birds, the soil, too, must be alive.

Come late May, strange denizens, forgotten since last summer, begin to emerge. One has changed remarkably little in forty million years. Around the edges of Maze Orchard, there has been little need to drain the land. If you're planting apple trees, rather than crops, you can be gentler on the soil – and in the sunlight-soaked depressions here lie crystal-clear, weed-filled ponds. Cut off from the nearby streams flowing through, these ponds are, naturally, fish-free – and that's exactly how the great-crested newt likes things to be.

Under the cover of darkness, these orange-eyed water dragons, dinosaur crests on their backs, become ever more adventuresome come the summer months. They sneak out of their ponds in search of new tadpoles to hunt – and lumber through the orchard, trying to evade capture by anything from a curious weasel to the small army of tawny owls, including now-fledged apprentices, hunting the apples each night. Twice, shining our torches speculatively across the orchard's forest floor, we have stumbled on these pocket dinosaurs as they head off on their strange and generally unseen journey through the trees.

The adjacent, old coppiced wood still has a thriving population of hazel dormice. As the lines of ancient hazel hedge extend into our adopted orchard, so too do these most adorable of rodents. By May, as deep twilight gives way to true night, you can, under a full moon, pick out the large black eyes that render these the 'cutest' animals in Britain. Dormice are not famed for high levels of activity; their name derives from the French word *dormir*, meaning to sleep. But as they creep and dart along hazel branches so narrow it seems inevitable they must fall off, night reveals a very different side to these arboreal trapeze-artists.

The dormice move with bursts of surprising speed – the fleet-footed terror of the wasp galls and aphids sheltering in the hazel's buckled limbs. When foraging, dormice cover large areas in a night; ceaselessly exploring, darting, searching, and as they scuttle through their hedgerow maze and move, seamlessly, into the wide, low branches of the apples close by, their plight in much of Britain becomes all too clear. Hazel dormice, like our lesser spotted woodpeckers, are not adapted to island life. They move through tree-lines, covering large areas yet never coming to ground. As the ancient outgrown hedgerows of Britain, which once joined our woodlands together as they still do here, have vanished, so the nocturnal highways of the countryside have closed.

As our dormouse gets its fill, and heads off for another

lengthy period of inaction, it occurs to us both that each year, we barely scratch the surface of the orchard's hidden world. In the night above, hundreds of unseen moth species will be flying. The larvae of one, the bark lichen-feeding *Dichomeris alacella*, has just been discovered by experts here this May. Prior to this, its larvae were unknown in our country. In the ground below, unseen nocturnal invertebrates will be crawling. We see only glimpses of the orchard's complex life. Its connections are complex, endless. Each visit unravels a dozen new threads.

The sobering thought is that studies into orchard diversity are only beginning – just as most ancient orchards are coming to an end. So are we, in truth, studying a dead habitat – a museum? Is this just a foray of curiosity? Ecological time-travel? A waste of time? We are all too aware that we are watching a habitat at the end of its life. We are recording a vanishing world that our grandchildren may never see. But as the tawny owlets screech and flop between the trees in Hop Kiln Orchard, scouring the young fruit trees amid the ancient grove – it doesn't feel that way. Instead, it feels like a beginning. How little we still know. How much there is still to save.

JUNE

FAMILY LIFE

NICK

*The informality of family life is a blessed
condition that allows us all to become our
best while looking our worst.*

MARGE KENNEDY

As the heart of summer approaches, the orchard's families are working full time. In the June frenzy to feed
and breed, species once secretive and reticent finally give
up all pretence of secrecy – as the life-or-death business
of feeding the family kicks in. During this most frenzied
of times, it's often the smallest stories that uncover the
biggest surprises.

Earlier each spring, as Ben and I clear out our nest boxes
ready for the upcoming season – evicting stowaway earwigs
and prospecting woodlice from flattened bales of moss and

feather – we routinely come across static black and yellow bodies, clamped to the inside walls of our man-made cavities. Bound using only their large mandibles, motionless wasp queens seem to favour these as their winter retreats – a safe place to sleep undisturbed through their hibernation. It doesn't appear much protection against a full British winter, but as they are able to survive being encased even in frost, it seems to do the trick. The queens of yellow-jackets and German wasps – the two species most likely to invite themselves to your summer picnic – are regulars, but once or twice a year we come across a far larger specimen: the slumbering giant of the wasp kingdom.

Here in the orchard, the blend of ageing fruit trees, diverse invertebrate life and a seasonal fruit glut create the ideal habitat for Britain's largest wasp species. At twice the size and over five times the weight of our common wasps, a queen European hornet is a formidable and impressive creature. Much maligned and unfairly feared, hornets are actually the pacifists of their tribe, rarely showing any interest in the activities of people and only ever stinging if cornered in a life-or-death situation. When finding these queens, we leave them be. But therein lies the mystery. For after this, between late March and early May, we rarely ever see a hornet. They don't appear to be brought in as prey by early nesting birds – and they aren't still hibernating. For all we know, they've emigrated.

But as reliably as the impending arrival of the summer equinox, a wander through the orchard in June always turns up one of these golden-banded bullets flying intently through the tree trunks, its purposeful head-height flight

Ancient Apples and Pensioner Pears. The oldest corner of our adopted orchard in winter. Cavities in every tree provide insulated shelter during freezing weather. © Nicholas Gates

The Modern 'Orchard'. Precisely planted for maximum productivity and ease of spraying, many orchards are now ecological deserts. © Paul Young / Alamy Stock Photo

A Vanishing World. A younger corner of the orchard in summer; the wood pasture landscape singing with life. © Nicholas Gates

Food Web. Six pairs of spotted flycatchers nest in the Hop Kiln Orchard gardens, raising their chicks on butterflies, bees, hoverflies and even hornets harvested from the orchard. © Benedict Macdonald

Life After Death. Freshly fallen deadwood fuels the orchard's extraordinary invertebrate diversity. © Nicholas Gates

On the Trail. A male rhinoceros beetle walks along pathways drilled out by many other beetle species in the orchard's abundant fallen timber. © Nicholas Gates

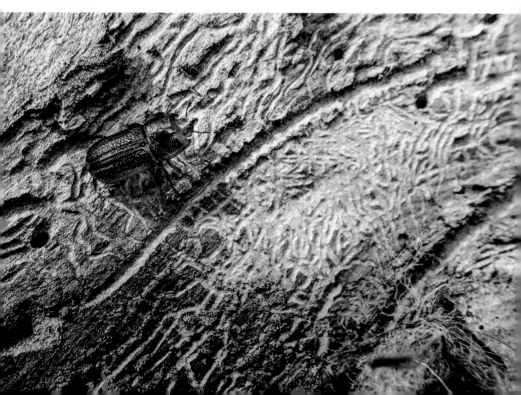

Blossoming. Perched amid lichens and apple blossom, a male redstart returns with a false click beetle after another successful orchard feeding foray. Myriad invertebrate species filling every niche ensure a healthy supply of prey for the orchard's many new mouths throughout the spring. © Nicholas Gates

Vanishing Act. Redstarts require well-concealed cavities for their carefully hidden nests. © Nicholas Gates

Indicator Species. Hornets play a key role in healthy orchard food chains, both the predator of invertebrates and the prey for birds and mammals. © Paul Harcourt Davies

Feeding Hatch. In a behaviour more famous among tropical hornbills, a male nuthatch passes food to his incubating mate through their clay front door.
© Nicholas Gates

Leaf Cradle. Just occasionally, nuthatches have opted to use our nest boxes, offering a rare glimpse of their eggs cocooned in a deep bowl of dried leaves.
© Benedict Macdonald

Underneath the Mistletoe. Nestled on top of an old mistle thrush nest, a brood of hungry song thrushes await their next delivery of organic worms. © Nicholas Gates

Tangled World. The cavities in the oldest orchard trees are spacious enough for tawny owls, barn owls and stock doves. They compete for prime nest holes with jackdaws, whose speckled blue-green eggs are always cradled in a sheep's wool nest. © Nicholas Gates

Jackdaw City. Prime cavities are metres deep with multiple entrance holes, yet even these ancient trees still produce a crop of fruit. Every one of these apartments is taken. © Nicholas Gates

Aerial Carpenters. Lesser spotted woodpeckers – a red-list species fast disappearing from Britain – thrive in the canopy deadwood left for them in the orchard. Each season, they drill multiple tiny nest holes, perfect homes for tits, rodents and beetles in future seasons. © Sam Hobson

Needle in a Haystack. The same size as a house sparrow, a female lesser spotted woodpecker blends in with the dappled bark of her blossoming apple tree.
© Nicholas Gates

Abundance. Blue tits and great tits are the most numerous of all the species that nest in the orchard. Their feeding forays harvest half a million caterpillars here each year. © Nicholas Gates

Nest Robbers. Starlings once regularly evicted great spotted woodpeckers from their cavities. The UK crash in starling numbers, caused by huge losses of their ground-dwelling prey, correlates with a boom in great spot numbers. © Nicholas Gates

The Surgical Carnivore. A great spotted woodpecker returns to its nest carrying the butchered remains of a great tit chick, hammered out from its nest cavity. Like hornets, these woodpeckers are voracious carnivores during their breeding season. © Nicholas Gates

The Lucky Ones. Tucked at the base of a rotting apple branch, this well-concealed great tit nest successfully avoided the orchard's great spotted woodpeckers. © Nicholas Gates

Prime Real Estate. The orchard is a fine place to rear a family. With space at a premium, nests turn up in all sorts of surprising places. This blackbird chose the inverted cavity of a fallen apple. © Nicholas Gates

Just Fitting In. Many species can thrive in human-shaped landscapes, as long as they have enough food. Generations of spotted flycatchers have been nesting in this same displaced-brick cavity for decades. © Nicholas Gates

The Autumnal Engine. In the 1970s, the huge old cider mill wheel was upgraded to petrol power in the form of a highly modified Matchless motorbike. It still works, but principally serves as a bottle store for the modern bottling line next door. © Nicholas Gates

Brock's Delight. During autumn, badgers make regular night-time raids on the windfall in the Hop Kiln Orchard garden. © Paul Hobson / naturepl.com

Winter Feast. During cold weather, abundant leftover fruit in orchards attracts thousands of migratory thrushes, finches and occasionally waxwings. © David Kjaer / naturepl.com

propelling it with the intent of a heat-seeking missile. Having ditched their springtime invisibility cloaks, hornets become easy to chase back to their nests as they return from their feeding forays. Following these hornet highways invariably turns up a lightning-scarred pear; one limb peeled off, allowing access to a rotting internal cavity. As the worker hornet disappears down a small, well-camouflaged hole, she highlights the masterpiece that her colony has sculpted.

Painted around the entrance hole is a kaleidoscope of natural paper – a mix of organic matter and hornet saliva – creating neatly woven strata of overlapping scales. This beige papier-mâché, built from pulped plant material, ranges in shade from pale sand through to amber ochre. Each hornet's addition is a slightly different shade to the last, like Van Gogh's brushstrokes in *The Starry Night*. Just a metre off the ground, this ephemeral artwork will last six months at best: a late autumn hailstorm will destroy its delicate framework, if an optimistic badger doesn't reach it first. But this isn't art for art's sake. It's a precision piece of engineering, crafted to deflect rainwater out of the cavity entrance while encouraging airflow. All of this is designed around a single entrance hole, in which a guard hornet waits on duty. It is entirely bespoke, meticulously built just for this one cavity – the only piece that will *ever* look like this. Each year, we look forward to finding these natural curiosities. The hornets' annual disappearing act is well worth the wait whenever we uncover this wild gallery with its sole exhibit.

When in full hunting mode, few invertebrates in the orchard are safe from these skilled predators. In 2018 – one of the hottest British summers on record – I watched in awe as one of these turbocharged wasps traumatised the large honeybee colony, hidden deep within the walls of the hop kiln. Its strategy was one of precision ambush; an avian leopard lying in wait. Positioning itself no more than a foot from the crack in the wall, the hornet waited – hovering deftly in mid-air – poised for a returning bee. The hornet seemed to know that honeybees arriving back from their forays burdened with pollen would be exhausted. It paid no attention to bees leaving *from* their hole in the crumbling mortar. Fresh-faced and unladen with pollen, they could readily escape its chasing jaws. But an exhausted bee, returning to its nest now up to 50 per cent heavier than before, is an entirely different matter.

Drifting gently in the air as if anchored to an invisible spider silk, the hornet sized up each incoming target. Some, it let pass. But when the hornet made its choice – and there was no going back – it aligned itself for a head-on crash. As the collision became imminent, the hornet spread its six legs, preparing landing gear that doubled as grappling hooks. Only at the last second did the bee react to this obstruction, banking hard up and away, as it overrode the powerful instinct driving it back to its nest. With a cheetah's turn of speed, the hornet fired upwards in pursuit. Pitching and rolling, a predatory Cirque de Soleil played out, as two species at the peak of their respective family trees clashed head to head. Despite an evasive backflip by the honeybee, six hornet legs soon enwrapped its exhausted body, drawing the chase to a swift conclusion as it was wrestled into a straightjacketed embrace. Setting a course for home, the hornet now steadied its new cargo, while proceeding to slice off the wings, abdomen and head. Only the honeybee's protein-rich flight muscles are taken back to a hornet's nest, to feed the dozens of larvae developing deep within their rotting, sculptured home.

Despite week after week of attacks like this, a healthy honeybee colony can withstand such summertime assaults, as long as they have abundant local nectar to feed from. Their tactic is simply to keep producing new brood. At the height of summer, a queen honeybee can be laying up to 1,500 eggs a day;[1] more than enough to withstand the predation of a few dozen lost each day to the hornets. But if the honeybees are stressed, either through insecticide poisoning or from their food source disappearing mid-season, the balance will soon tip the other way.

While the honeybees run the daily gauntlet of hornet bulldogs, the many different species of solitary bee in the orchard face an altogether different challenge. If a comic artist tried to come up with a superhero nemesis, they'd do well to improve on the lethal weaponry of one of Britain's largest parasitic insects.

Picture an incredibly lanky wasp, its wiry frame coated in glossy black. Out-of-place muscular thighs power dainty tapering legs, the tip of each dipped in brilliant white. When at rest, propped up on white stilettos, long wings meet neatly on its fine elongated back. Pert straight antennae mechanically twitch as if someone had forgotten to switch them off, giving the impression of a creature permanently on edge. A flash of red along the abdomen provides a subtle warning that this creature has an ulterior motive. And its tail is in a league of its own. Most bees and wasps have tapered bottoms, but the rear end of the imposingly-named *Gasteruption jaculator* is the stuff of nightmares, armed with a slender sheathed needle longer than its own body, giving it the appearance of a flying hypodermic syringe. If Mary Shelley had ever met *Gasteruption*, Frankenstein might have turned out very differently. This is a specialist parasite, its oversized organ responsible for penetrating the well-concealed nests of solitary bees and wasps. But before *Gasteruption* can put her weapon to good use, the female first has to find her quarry.

Lodged in bankside earthworm tunnels, brick wall crevices and particularly old beetle larvae borings around the orchard, a wide array of solitary bees are busy provisioning little egg chambers and then boxing in their next generation. But each time a female solitary bee goes out to forage for pollen, her home is left exposed. This is when *Gasteruption* strikes. It might seem like an impossible task as a five-centimetre-long insect flies around the orchard searching for the tiny entrance hole to a solitary bee nest. But this parasite comes armed with a military-grade toolkit. Her eyes are primed to search for likely pieces of deadwood among the fruit groves, while those large thighs are actually precision calculators – filled with muscles that are able to pinpoint the subtlest vibrations emitted by larvae below the bark she lands on. She may even be able to smell the chemicals emitted by feeding larvae.[2] And to top it off, *Gasteruption* is already attached to the needle in *this* haystack.

Watching her slowly fly around the trees, it is surprising

how efficiently her prospecting returns a likely site. Antennae flick furiously as she crawls around her chosen tunnel, front legs remaining poised to detect the cavity wall that she knows hides her hosts. As long as she avoids meeting the hole's owner – which usually results in a swift retreat – *Gasteruption* can deploy her secret weapon. In the pitch darkness of the solitary bee's nest, and using her abdomen to align her biological syringe, *Gasteruption* is able to locate the bee's larva, pierce its skin without killing it, and impregnate it with one of her own eggs. Other eggs she will place among the brood. By the time the female solitary bee returns to provision her young, *Gasteruption* has left without any trace she had ever visited at all.

Only weeks later will the nightmarish reality of *Gasteruption*'s visit become apparent to the solitary bees unfortunate enough to have been singled out for surgery. Breaking out of the skin of the unwitting, hapless and now very dead solitary bee larva, baby *Gasteruption* rapidly gets to work munching its way through the rest of the solitary bee's larval brood. Insatiable, it will consume them all – and then, it will consume their pollen too. Eating the bee out of house and home, *Gasteruption* will then spend the entire winter within the bee's stolen apartment.[3] Then, from next May, and into September, a new generation of flying syringes will emerge – to wreak domestic havoc on the orchard's hardworking solitary bees.

A repetitive, high-pitched '*tsree, tsree*' vibrato emanates from the branches, like tiny fluting windchimes tinkling in the breeze. The treecreeper – its call as distinctive as it is subtle – is a woodland specialist, armed with a sickle-shaped beak to winkle out small beetle grubs, spiders and wood-boring moth larvae from the folds and flakes in the bark.

While woodpeckers are the engineers of the orchard, the treecreepers are its dentists. By cleaning out any wood-feeding invertebrates – their fine beaks working like dental floss in the narrow gaps – they help retard decay from setting in. Which is ironic, as to safely raise a family, that is exactly what these intricately patterned little birds need. Combing a corner of the Oak Orchard one afternoon, while being taunted by the faint tinkling trill of a treecreeper hopping around the branches, I decided to methodically work through each tree and uncover where this secretive dental surgeon was nesting. The search was soon narrowed down to one; a squat and concave old apple, wider than it was tall. It was one of those trees defying its own demise, naturally hollowed out but somehow still producing a single healthy leaf-filled branch. With no peeling outer bark obvious, the nest could only be hidden inside the arced wall of the tree, a shallow crumbling skin of weatherbeaten sapwood now measuring no more than a hand's-width in depth.

The old West Country name for a treecreeper is the 'tree mouse' – which perfectly describes their scuttling dashes as they spiral up their chosen foraging tree. Outside of the nesting season, monogamous treecreeper pairs work together, the female routinely scouring the upper parts of the trees while her mate examines the lower parts. When feeding, their oversized feet and extra-stiff tail feathers form a rigid platform when pressed against bark; a tripod from which they can lever out difficult prey. Their quiet chatter keeps them constantly updated as to the other's whereabouts, and signals when it's time to up sticks and butterfly-flit to the base of the next tree. But now with a nest to attend to, brooded only by his mate, the male must provide for the family.

Yet even watching him return to the tree, it was unclear just *where* he was taking his beak full of pulped beetle grubs and mangled spiders. He was remarkably unfazed by my presence, but only after moving for the third time did I notice the tiny sliver of rotting wood that this avian Houdini was managing to squeeze behind. Seams of black rot added a rich texture to the decay, creating an illusion that concealed this natural hidden door; a gap less than two centimetres wide. Inspecting this port revealed just one angle that allowed a window in. Out of the darkness, a beady jet-black eye returned my gaze; the dappled ochre, ivory and pale black patchwork on the back of this brooding female treecreeper keeping her well camouflaged as she stared down the giant intruder peering in. Intricately moulded into this shallow gap, she was perched atop the smallest nest I have ever seen: a little bowl built from the finest wood shavings, lined with lichen and varnished with spider silk.

Treecreepers have one of the smallest eggs of all British species, even tinier than that laid by a wren. Despite this, after hatching the chicks grow immensely fast on their protein-rich diet of pulped invertebrates and are able to fledge in record time; as few as twelve days. It's over this period that they display their most endearing characteristic, because for the first week of their flying lives they never lose sight of each other. Apparently refusing to embrace the free world, they instead choose to replicate the cramped confines of their tiny nest everywhere they move, shuffling up tree trunks together in a roving crèche – never wanting to be left out of the huddle. When this camouflaged doily stops, the chicks hang like shingle scales off the trunks of the orchard trees, well-hidden so long as they remain still. With seven new apprentices joining the orchard dental service, the trees here would now be given a light respite from the glut of small invertebrates feasting in their boughs.

In spring, the orchard's damp 'orange-tip' meadow sizzled with the smell of wild garlic, but by the start of summer its scented verdure is replaced with a visual mosaic, domi-nated by symmetrical lilac crowns. Dainty creeping thistles, with their small pom-pom turrets, are shadowed by their larger cousins, flat-topped spear thistles – their spiky orb-like receptacles propping up a canopy of vertical, pointed petals. Resistant to all but the most determined herbivores, thistles provide a welcome influx of nectar as the inverte-brate breeding season reaches its peak.

Dozens of bumblebee, solitary bee and butterfly species work their way between this thorny food source, yet every so often a more unusual species flies gracefully past. With lustrous black wings adorned with badges of red spots, flashing to a bright metallic green as it catches the light, and blood-red underwings bordered with the finest of black margins, burnet moths are unmistakable as they flutter slowly among the grasses and thistles. Of the half-dozen similar-looking species found in Britain, the six-spot burnet is the most commonly encountered in this particular meadow. Their conspicuous colouration is no accident, for as caterpillars, the infants of these day-flying moths are alchemists. As they munch their way through the leaves of bird's-foot trefoil, they are able to sequester poisonous compounds from this petite yellow-flowered plant into a lethal concentration of hydrogen cyanide. Bright warning colours are the burnet moth caterpillars' way of permanently broadcasting an honest meal review, indicating to potential predators that this dinner is truly dreadful, and it really is in *their* interests to go and find lunch elsewhere. But this isn't the cyanide's sole purpose.

Once fully grown, six-spot burnet moth caterpillars set out on a vertical expedition. Selecting a tall sturdy grass stem, they crawl their way up from the tangled melee of wildflowers high into the draughty world above. Skilfully weaving a straw-coloured cocoon using a special silk gland near their mouth, they camouflage this temporary home to blend exactly with a widening in the grass stalk. A few weeks later, the adult moth emerges; vibrantly coloured and plump with toxins. This is where their story moves from the interesting to the extraordinary.

As the freshly-hatched female moth flies amid the meadow, searching not just for food but for a mate, she emits a fine vapour trail of cyanide. These noxious mist clouds are infused with her pheromones, in just a high enough dose for the males to seek them out without being grounded by the poison in the process. As she intersperses her flying with pauses on the nearest vantage point, it's not uncommon to come across a female moth surrounded by a posse of suitors, all crowded atop a prominent spear thistle. Sitting watching these moth parties, it's astonishing to realise that the cyanide so poisonous to our own bodies is vital to their survival. Yet the more we understand the complexity of the orchard's life, and the surprising and secretive species that call it home, the more we realise, each summer, how rare and imperilled this orchard island is for the inhabitants that call it home.

Rhinoceros beetles are unmistakable. With a single horn, this metallic black beetle looks like a tiny Triceratops dinosaur. As they bulldoze their way into pea-sized breeding tunnels to lay their own eggs, it's not uncommon to find the rear end of one poking out of a scarred orchard tree, as an overly protective male sits guard over his mate inside. Boring trails into the wood like this, they create miles of micro-habitats for other animals; everything from spider bolt-holes to potential wooden caves for solitary bees.

But there is one beetle that lives in these orchard trees that is rarer than all others. Among entomologists, the noble chafer is beetle royalty, only seen by a handful of the most dedicated searchers. An iridescent British racing green with a lightly wrinkled carapace and a gentle dusting of pale hairs on its underside, we have never actually set eyes on an adult noble chafer here. Its rarity is predominantly due to its rather fussy preference for a particular type of dead-wood. Or more specifically, the food choice of its larva – for it spends over 90 per cent of its lifecycle as a fat, pale-cream grub, boring its way through the decaying heart-wood of old fruit trees. Hidden deep within the rotting limbs of mature fruitwood, we only know of its presence from its 'frass' – the beetle larvae's poo – that fills up many of the older woodpecker cavities and rot-holes here.

The reason that noble chafers are now found almost exclusively in ancient orchards in this region of Britain is, in part, due to our long-standing obsession with tidying the wider landscape, over centuries, of its open-grown trees and fallen veterans. Today, connected networks of wild fruit trees have been lost from most of our wooded areas except the New Forest. And as ancient fruiting trees have disap-peared over centuries from the wider landscape, species like noble chafers, reliant on deadwood and decay, have found sanctuary in these oldest of orchards; accidental nature reserves in an ever-more sanitised countryside.

For the majority of the year, great spotted woodpeckers are a welcome sight; a bright flash of colour on a crisp winter's day, or the dawn backing track to a spring wood-land walk. Even as they gatecrash lesser spotted woodpecker excavation attempts in April and May, forcing their smaller

cousins to start again, we begrudgingly tolerate their bellig-
erence, as we set about re-finding the new homes of lesser
spotted woodpeckers. But in June, the great spotted woodpecker's behaviour worsens from delinquent to murderous,
as these much-loved birds develop a taste for *flesh*. Now,
with ruthless efficiency, great spotted woodpeckers begin
to target the nests of the orchard's cavity specialists.
Carefully refined through millions of years of evolution,
they are already equipped with the tools to find and extract
growing chicks from the most well-hidden of nests.

In 2016, however, the great spots really let themselves
down. Of all the common blue- and great-tit prey freely
available in the orchard – the great spots chose instead to
scoff the nestlings of our cherished lesser spotted woodpeckers. Drawn by the piercing begging calls of the tiny
chicks, the male great spot alighted beside the tiny nest
– and soon, his female followed. Rather than enlarging the
nest hole itself, they shimmied down until they could hear
the chicks deep within the cavity. Then, they began to dig
them out. Surgical drill-like bills made short work of the
soft, dead wood. We watched, helplessly, as the tiny adult
lesser spots launched frenzied attacks on their larger cousins,
only to be rebuffed – or ignored. And the attack's duration
only made it more painful. Only one chick was taken at a
time. Whenever it seemed like the assault was over, the
parents pitifully resumed trying to feed their remaining
chicks. And then, ten minutes later, the executioner would
return; plucking the next tiny chick from the now ripped-
open nest cavity. This continued until all the chicks were
gone. Even then, the adult lesser spots were left at the nest

site, hopefully inspecting the wreckage to triple-check, in vain, for any last survivor.

Why, given the abundance of insect life in June, do great spotted woodpeckers become avian carnivores? Our clearest answer yet came one afternoon as we sat watching a small screen monitor, tucked below an ancient, tumbledown cherry. The image was being relayed from a remote camera, clamped four metres up in a mature apple, and showed the active nest of a pair of great spotted woodpeckers, drilled into the damp rot in the shadow of a particularly large bracket fungus.

Ben had found the nest just a day earlier, pinpointed thanks to the chicks' impulsive begging calls. For up to ten days before they fledge, young great spotted woodpeckers get particularly excitable, jostling for position in their increasingly crowded cavern. On a hot day, the temperature and humidity generated by four chicks in something the volume of a large walking sock must get particularly unbear-able, so they regularly clamber up to their entrance hole, poking their heads out to try and cool off. Between panting, the chicks emit a steady chatter of calls to remind mum and dad to come and feed them; audible now from over twenty metres away.

The goal was to photograph the parents feeding the chicks at the entrance hole – and to see what food was coming in. A finger was poised over the remote trigger as the familiar and subtle 'kek' call signalled that a food delivery was imminent. A dish of spider, perhaps? A smörgåsbord of beetle larvae? Instead, as a flashy red rump dropped into shot, offsetting the crisp white underside of an adult male great spot, the bird's prey choice was altogether more surprising. Clenched in the woodpecker's beak was a *leg*: a miniature drumstick. I burst off a volley of shots as the mouthful was enthusiastically but awkwardly devoured by one of his waiting chicks. As the male bird silently popped off the tree, his chicks continued their murmur. Less than a minute later, he was back – this time carrying another drumstick: presumably the *other* leg. This scene repeated itself as a torso and then a whole head arrived. This made the unfortunate victim easy to identify – a young great tit around twelve days old. The speed with which the adult was returning to the nest indicated that somewhere nearby, he had wedged the unfortunate young bird in a tree cleft: a natural butcher's board that allowed it to be diced into manageable mouthfuls.

Switching diet for just a few weeks each year, great spots are able to give their growing chicks a valuable protein boost; a bodybuilder's diet for their final few weeks in the nest. While a big caterpillar can weigh up to a gram, a young great tit is at least ten times that, and already contains exactly the right blend of protein, fat and important minerals, such as calcium, that the young great spotted woodpeckers need to transition from innocent nestlings to heavyweight nest raiders.

Throughout the orchard, as the blue tits, great tits, coal tits, treecreepers and lesser spotted woodpeckers work hard to find myriad caterpillars, spiders, bark beetles and other insects for their young families, up to three pairs of great spotted woodpeckers track their nest efforts – timing their daytime raids to perfection and precisely extracting large chicks. Each time they do, another useable nest cavity is destroyed.

Such predations, of course, are nothing new. What has changed in recent years, however, is a growing imbalance within our woodland food-chains – and in the orchard itself. Once, great spotted woodpeckers had a nemesis of their own. Starlings, even more than sparrowhawks, are nature's most effective means of controlling great spotted woodpecker numbers. They aggressively compete with, and generally win against great spots; stealing their nests and forcing them to excavate a new one. This, in turn, limits the productivity of the larger woodpeckers, because they must then nest again. Often, by such a time, food supplies are no longer optimal for feeding their chicks.

Such 'control' mechanisms can still be seen commonly in places like eastern Poland, where starlings thrive and continue to terrorise great spotted woodpeckers each spring, robbing them of their zealously crafted log cabins. But starlings have vanished, in recent decades, from most of our woodlands and many of our orchards. Their food supplies, crawling in the soil, have vanished too, as chemicals such as avermectins, used to worm cattle, have toxified the soil, reducing the abundance of earthworm and leatherjacket prey. Overtrampling by livestock has made the starling's remaining food ever harder to access.[4] And as starlings have vanished, great spotted woodpeckers have become one of the most prolific nest predators of our woodlands.

Having increased by 800 per cent in recent decades, the species has, across Britain, been observed not only to predate the nests of lesser spotted woodpeckers, but is responsible for seven of every ten predations on the nests of willow tits, whose dead, stumpy homes are devastatingly easy to excavate.[5] The greatest densities of willow tits, now found in northern counties like Durham, are generally found where large numbers of great spotted woodpeckers have yet to build up.

As we watch each year the considerable carnivory of the woodpeckers in the orchard, it is another reminder to us of how fragile this orchard's island ecosystem is. Our adopted orchard, like the countryside at large, is now tipping out of balance; its inhabitants and their lives becoming more and more out of kilter with the rhythms that once governed the countryside. And we fear that even here, in these most biodiverse and unspoilt of fruit forests, we are losing, or have already lost a whole cast of species that once called these places home.

JULY

LOST WORLDS

BEN

Nine bean-rows will I have there,
a hive for the honey-bee,
And live alone in the bee-loud glade.

WILLIAM BUTLER YEATS

'Flying deer!' My guide wasn't pointing at a Christmas card. Black and blood-red, the antlered giant took to the air. It was the most improbable take-off I had seen. Anyone who has watched ungainly bustards take flight, or even pollen-fattened bumble bees lumbering through the garden, defying the laws of physics as we know them, would have shared my sense of disbelief. The male stag beetle, the size of a matchbox – and about as ungainly in flight – hummed through the orchard air and landed, or smacked, into a gnarly old pear. Rob, the owner of the orchard, was unfazed. 'He is looking for a mate,' he said. 'As the sun goes down, soon there will be dozens on the wing. The night is warm.'

Stag beetles are one of nature's more extreme creations. They have sacrificed a great deal in order to wrestle with other males for the right to mate. Their enormous mandibles, or 'antlers', can account for around a fifth of their entire body weight. Running is unstable and costs the males 40 per cent more energy than females. In spite of their impressive appearance, stag beetles are fragile indeed. Short-lived giants, males will survive for just a few weeks as adults, as they awkwardly cruise the airspace of Europe's old-growth woodlands in search of a mate. In this fleeting window, size matters. The larger the mandible, the more chance a male has of deftly flipping his opponent off a rotten branch. His is the life of a sumo wrestler, where weight plus timing brings victory.

Yet the greatest threat to stag beetles is not being unceremoniously uprooted and chucked off a log. Over centuries, they have vanished across much of Europe – and from most of Britain. Stag beetles are Europe's invertebrate equivalent of elephants. Giants among their kin, 'winged deer' demand much from the landscape around them. Their disappearance tells a story of change. Like so much of Europe's vanishing wildlife, stag beetles inhabit decaying, ancient places. Their demands extend not only into the future, but deep into the past. Habitats must have remained undisturbed for many years indeed, if stag beetles are to thrive. These giants are the product of time in trees.

Up to seven years of the winged deer's long life cycle is spent as a pupa, submerged deep within dead or decaying wood. Ancient, open-grown oaks, cherries, apples, pears, willows and black poplars – some of these almost ghost trees in our ordered modern landscapes – form invaluable rotting residences. Stag beetle larvae feed only on decaying wood. They have no use for live trees. The adults lay their eggs in rotting timber, and so the more standing dead trees in the landscape, the better. Log piles, left in older orchards or gardens, can also recreate the beneficial chaos once left in the wake of a disruptive herbivore. It is often here that stag beetles will emerge come early July.

Lying quietly in this orchard as the sun goes down, more and more stags can be discerned. Gliding like airborne tanks, they weave the mottled, furrowed maze of the old pear trees. As the orchard turns orange, a late swallowtail, as it may have done centuries ago in our own country, glides around the apple blossoms. The deep thrum of turtle doves vies with cuckoo staccato. My journey has been worthwhile. It feels for a moment as if I have cheated time. I am sitting in an ancient Hungarian orchard, on the very southern tip of Europe's Carpathian mountains. I am here to enjoy a spectacle which has vanished from much of Europe, and is vanishing worldwide: a supercharged abundance of insect life. Indeed, the perseverance of insect *superabundance*, here in the Carpathians, lies at odds with most of western Europe and much of the temperate western world.

The Carpathians also contain the largest areas of traditional orchards remaining in Europe. Indeed, almost every village in many areas might be regarded as one continuous orchard. The entire farmland system here, growing ever wilder and richer in orchards as you enter Romania, recalls a method of using the land, and an abundance of insects, perhaps not seen in Britain for well over two centuries. The rural-heavy communities in these regions, still living off the land, maintain their gardens not for show but for practical self-sustenance and fruit growing. As such, the distinction between a garden and an orchard becomes almost redundant. Gardens here *are* orchards – and I am here to see Europe's orchard world at its very best.

The Saly orchard and its surrounding farmlands and woodlands, a place I had visited for a number of summers, has been described by one naturalist as being home to 'British wildlife on steroids'. Here, few bat an eyelid at the evening spectacle of 'flying deer'. No one tries to count the volume of cuckoos or turtle doves; two of the commonest birds that sing and feed in the orchard. No one has issued an action plan to save a traditional orchard. Indeed, few of the local Hungarian or Romani people here would recognise an intensive British orchard; its straight boughs thin with song and thick with toxins.

From this orchard, north into Slovakia, then east into Ukraine and, finally, south again into Romania, a satellite view of Europe would reveal an alluring horseshoe of deep green. Here live wolves, bears, lynx – and thriving communities of people: the farmlands here are still rich in farmers. This orchard, with its tree sparrows, wrynecks and stag beetles, loud with bees and dancing with butterflies, is unremarkable. From here, for hundreds of kilometres into

Slovakia and Romania, you will find a thousand little orchards like this one.

Anyone travelling to the far reaches of eastern Europe, with its older way of managing the countryside, will find that the remarkable soon becomes the everyday. Nightingales adorn almost every dense stand of roses in the orchard hedgerow. On each nettle, you come to expect not one caterpillar or two, but a thick black swarm of peacock caterpillars. Newspapers might call this an infestation. Most of us have forgotten that a nettle should be at least half black. Black poplars, of which just four hundred remain in Britain, grow and die in groves beside the villages. Fluting with unseen orioles, no one has thought to cut them down. From their girth, many must be hundreds of years old – they stand because no one has noticed, nor thought to make way for a metre's more yield of corn.

While none of us alive can remember swallowtails dancing along the roadsides of southern England, you soon become accustomed to them gliding down the lanes and around the orchards here, pausing to sip nectar from apple blossom as they go. Endangered rarities in much of western Europe, and lost to Britain, large copper butterflies, flashing their scarlet wings, thrive beside the orchard; not in fens but in damp ditches. Black-veined whites are among the commonest of orchard butterflies; their caterpillars raised on fruit trees, the adults with a fondness for thistles.

Unfettered by the genetic bottlenecks that have caused so many British butterflies to become tied to just a few food-plants, many butterflies in this ancient corner of Europe have never faced the population fragmentation that forces them into specialised habitats, managed at great cost. All share the same landscape. Birds lost to England, too, have yet to become rare. No one has told the orchard-nesting red-backed shrikes that they are supposed to specialise in heathland. Village house martins come by the two-hundred. Yet for all this glorious mayhem, the roadsides carry cars, the houses are inhabited, the gardens are gardened, and the grasslands and orchards are farmed. This is a very *human* paradise.

One of the reasons that this part of eastern Europe remains so extraordinarily rich is that it still adopts farming practices not seen in England for almost three hundred years. In terms of agricultural profits, then, it is *poor* by the standards of Britain's farming unions. Farms are small. Food is grown to feed local people. The Carpathian countryside is less of a factory and more of a gently tilled garden. As such, it holds room for infinite nuance, such as the rotting willow stands or the copper-lit wetlands at the edges of the farmland.

There is no doubt that rural poverty has played some role in keeping things this way. The farms are small and scruffy, in part because they do not have the funds to be big and tidy. The creeping menace of the Common Agricultural Policy and its factory economics have thankfully yet to take root. Most houses here now have one car. But as you push north into Slovakia and Romania, many of those cars will disappear. Deep within the mountains, in some Romanian villages, the pavements are thick with purple emperors and house martins, in part because those villages' economies are still powered by horse and cart. Winged life throngs to the insect-rich dung that the horses deposit in the streets.

Yet it would be unfair to put the stewardship of this gently farmed paradise down to poverty alone, especially in Hungary, where the quality of life is often good. Here, in the villages around the orchard, many live comfortable lives. Doctors, teachers and many other professionals are not farmers, but return home from work to their jumbled, wild gardens each evening. These homesteads are, though, far more self-sufficient than many in England – and this self-sufficiency is reflected in the landscape as a whole. Here lies a comfortable sharing arrangement with wildlife, which others might do well to study and adopt.

Mature orchards are not living museums, protected as nods to a crumbling past, but practical growing areas that nobody has thought to tidy or cut down. Orchards join up, mile after village mile, to provide deciduous wood pastures; connected not by wild forests but busy villages. This became apparent one morning as I climbed to the highest of the Bukk Hills – and looked down. Each village was a sea of green: houses jostled with trees. To the tidy-trained British eye, it looked as if each small town had been 'swallowed' by a sea of leaves. From even this distance, the chorus of birds could be heard: the *'choo-choo-choo'* of garden night-ingales as persistent as the sound of church bells.

One other factor here is a quiet awareness of the natural world, shared by many who live within the countryside. In Britain, I have met many 'country people' (though by no means all) who can barely separate the birds on their own farms, much as many would claim some deep connection with the countryside. In interesting contrast, it is said by many naturalists in Hungary that the local Romani retain an uncanny knack for finding any wild animal in the wood-lands and farmlands around their homes. Not only do they appear each morning with baskets of edible mushrooms, but they have, in the past, tracked fire salamanders or the first emerging poplar admirals in the woodlands around these villages for naturalists. This generational contract with the countryside has, perhaps, never been broken at all.

Alongside an understanding of what lives where, of how nature *shares*, comes greater tolerance of nature on the doorstep. Log piles, untidy to the British eye, adorn every garden: the peoples of the Carpathian villages create more hedgehog habitat by accident than Britain's conservationists do by design. Wildflower diversity is a universal expression of village life. Ramshackle fruit trees, far more useful than decking, also prove more valuable come the autumn. Muddy wet areas beside streams, the precious building yards of house martins, are as common in these villages as decaying trees and attic bats. By contrast a mown verge, for the working farmland people of these villages, would seem a costly extravagance. So would rodenticides or insec-ticides, given the thriving populations of cuckoos, bats and owls that haunt each village.

The orchard village system here in the Carpathians is deeply practical. People and wildlife thrive. After a few days staying with Rob, he whisked me down into the wine cellar. Here, shivering in silence, like an eerie carpet of gravity-defying leaves, an uncountable colony of lesser horseshoe bats watched with mild disapproval from the ceiling. Rob deftly and quietly picked up a dusty bottle of Egri Bikaver, mumbled his apologies – and left. 'They put up with us, we put up with them,' said Rob simply. 'They poo all over my wine bottles. I give them a home – so, they have to put up with me, too.' This, in so many ways, defines the sharing arrangement still present in this part of farmed Europe. The bats, of course, provide an invaluable service in Rob's orchard, too; flickering up the stairwell and out through a small window to cleanse the orchard's pest species by night.

In Britain, our forgotten ability to live alongside most wildlife, most of the time, has rendered lesser horseshoes, like so many species, museum pieces more than living beasts with whom we share the countryside. Our inability to share human spaces with nature has ironically been matched only by our ability to create statutes of 'thou shalt not', in order to protect the last survivors. In Britain, it is a crime to set eyes on a colony of these bats in an attic without a licence, yet it appears these bats' Hungarian cousins do not implode upon brief visual examination. What lesser horse-shoes actually need, apart from dank 'cave' cellars, is not an absence of humans – but a fluttering abundance of prey. This became readily apparent as we opened the Bull's Blood, a rich red wine from the vineyards of these hills – and set a candle in a jar on the table.

Just as the orchard had been bee-loud by day, the thud and scuffle of moths and night-flying beetles attained invasion proportions by night. White ermines, elephant hawk-moths and soon, spectacular emperors, angry false eyes flashing on their wings, swept down around us. Moths to a flame, it turns out, is still a serious issue for those dining outside in this older part of Europe. We snuffed the candle and decamped with our goulash, and our wine, inside. To the night, we left a fluttering frenzy of moths sufficient to feed colonies of lesser horseshoe bats that, in this village alone, number into their thousands.

The following morning, the dawn chorus literally gets me out of bed. One voice dominates – and for all his poetic brilliance, Browning didn't listen closely enough.

That's the wise thrush . . .
He sings each song twice over,
Lest you think he could never recapture,
The first fine careless rapture!

Song thrushes, however, sing their core refrain not twice, but thrice. They occasionally loop the odd phrase, but the unique ascending volley of two notes hits the airwaves on three rapidly repeated occasions. In one small section of allotments, predominantly pears and cherries, as many as twenty birds are competing. But it isn't just song that thrushes hammer out.

While beetles, butterflies and moths have dozens of avian predators, snails have rather fewer. A range of thrush species worldwide can open smaller snails, but only song thrushes specialise in the size of snails that lead to clammy, sleepless nights for Britain's legions of keen gardeners. As with any bird which has adopted a unique feeding behaviour – like the cuckoos that can swallow hairy caterpillars, only to eject the toxic hairs later on – the song thrush's evolution suggests it has spent many millennia adapting to crush these common garden pests. Nothing brings a snail out of its shell like a song thrush.

The song thrush grabs its snail of choice and then carries it some distance to an 'anvil' rock – or another equally hard place. Here, it will bash the snail's shell into smithereens and impale the quaking morsel inside. Over the years, ornithologists have watched blackbirds try to copy the same technique – but with remarkably little success.

As the thrush war continues overhead, I start to look around at the state of the cabbages. Even here, in a land fizzing with likely pests, they look remarkably pristine. A few large white caterpillars are hard at work – but the damage of a snail army is hard to detect. Here in the orchard, snails are slow-moving refugees. If they cross the orchard lawn to the cabbage patch, a migration of a good twenty minutes, then an army of thrushes lies in wait – their favourite anvil perhaps already in their minds.

Strange too, for a moment, is the absence of slugs. You will meet many gardeners, even naturalists, who fail to recognise the importance of slugs to the European food-chain. But that is because slugs, like their predators, are nocturnal. I am keen to prove my guesses as to why Rob's cabbages are in such good shape. That evening, I sit quietly by the cabbage patch as the sun falls. I can't see the slugs in the dark, but soon there comes the snuffle, shuffle, so common even in my childhood – and so dearly missed. In Britain, I haven't seen one in a year. My grandchildren may never see one at all – so I try not to take it for granted. Nor the *half a dozen* hedgehogs that follow.

The orchard's bristled battalion does not move rapidly – nor does it need to. Their prey is hardly fast-moving. Slugs and snails stand little chance, and beetles, another vanishing prey item for Britain's hedgehogs, will be assiduously rooted out of wood piles. The hedgehog's feared predator, the badger, is not common in this better-balanced part of the European ecosystem. Badger cubs are predated by lynx and wolves, and they naturally have lower densities in the heavily wooded habitats of eastern Europe. By contrast, the denuded pasture farmlands of upland Britain may hold the world's highest concentration of badgers. Here in Hungary, badgers are neither in charge – nor are they common. The orchard hedgehog patrol marches on.

Soon, hearing a snorting slurp, I'm fairly sure my hog of choice has found its first slug of the night. It's now hard to keep track of how many hedgehogs are emerging from their log piles. As they scuffle around, it occurs to me that between here and Romania, there is perhaps not one slug-pellet, concrete decked garden or impenetrable garden fence. The hedgehogs have the run not just of villages, but village after village – able to move, shelter and find food throughout the human farmland maze.

While hedgehogs seek out the drier quarters in the myriad log piles here, the wet rooms are favoured by another player in the slug-hunting equation. My unprofessional amusement at the movement of toads, which has never left me since childhood, is unlikely to be shared by the orchard's slow-moving procession of slugs. Common toads are one of the slug's most deadly predators – and on a damp evening the orchard is thick with both. I watch as they head off with purposeful intent into the gloom, slowly tracking their glacial prey. Here in the orchard's jumbled habitats, little freshwater ponds are perfectly suited to amphibians. From around them, toads go on little nocturnal sallies not unlike Africa's hippos – eating voraciously as they go.

Toads, like frogs, are readily taken for granted. Yet Britain has lost almost 70 per cent of its toads in the past thirty years – a loss of hundreds of thousands. The lives of the world's amphibians, too, have never been under greater threat. Over half of them now face extinction; higher than any other animal group. Common toads love smaller, deeper water-bodies; but many of these, whether village or farm-land ponds, have become increasingly unsuitable in Britain. Farmland drainage has desiccated many pools. Others have filled with the run-off from fertilisers, which can interfere with tadpole development. Increasingly, at the more local level, fewer of us have ponds in our gardens. Road traffic, a light affair here in Hungary, can disrupt entire migrations in Britain, effectively cutting off whole wetlands. Toads remind us how little nature needs to survive – yet quite how much we have been capable of taking away.

People often think 'big' when talking of ecosystem regu-lation. Wolves regulate deer. Bears regulate a range of animals by killing their young, including boar. Big herbivores, like tree-breaking bison, can have a profound impact on the richness and shape of a grassland. Yet it is in the tiny lives of orchards, farms and villages, perhaps, of our smallest neighbours, that we begin to comprehend the enormous impacts of the *smaller* animals beside us.

England's gardeners use slug-pellets, at cost, because they

are short of hedgehogs, toads and song thrushes. Many can no longer enjoy the life-giving energy that these animals bring to their doorsteps – nor can they savour the quality and taste of a toad-patrolled cabbage patch. As the village barn owl floats through the orchard, off to harvest the surplus rodents that could plague the village if unchecked, it all seems rather obvious that nature is on hand to help – and that orchards are one such place where the symbiosis of *us* and *them* works best of all.

The following morning, the toads have sloped off. Now, the orchard pond is humming a new tune. It looks at first glance as if the water is frothing: its surface is thick with drinking honeybees. In tiny feats of static defiance, their legs test the water's skin, their proboscises snatch a tiny droplet – and off they go. In the course of such a raid, a large hive of bees can drink 12 litres of water in a *day*. Bees do not just need water in the way that we do – to regulate our cells, temperature and brain function. Water helps bees to dissolve crystallised honey in their hives, which, if too viscous and thick, becomes problematic to ingest come the lean winter months. Rob tells me there are five million bees in hives around the orchard and the village. I presume he means five thousand – but we pop around to see the local beekeeper. 'No,' he tells us, 'I have around five million bees. And,' he adds, with a puzzled look at my doubting face, 'why not?'

In a village where the air is clear, nectar omnipresent, verges untrimmed and meadows cut for silage only at the very end of summer; where no chemicals cloud the bees' judgement nor plague their minds; where little ponds lie everywhere, bees are loud. To the western ear, the hum I hear would best be likened to a motorway. Perhaps few people alive in our own country have ever heard bees *roar*.

The impact of this humming army on the orchard and village is profound. In the verges, wildflowers of every imaginable variety vie with one another for space. In place of the nitrate-fuelled rye grasses we find growing rank beside many British roadsides, devil's bit scabious, verbena, bird's foil trefoil, wild carrot and a dozen other flowers contest one square metre of disturbed earth. The flowers' buzzing envoys carry their nectar far and wide. Every orchard edge is a riot. Now, as the sun comes out, the cream-whites of *Umbelliferae* flowers shiver under a wing-flexing carpet of heath fritillaries. Within the orchard, the roar grows louder. On close inspection, almost every apple blossom has a pollinating bee. Nature's fundamental feedback loops, as in so many parts of the Carpathians, remain intact.

The sheer abundance and diversity of life, within the tiniest of spaces, becomes increasingly hard to comprehend as the sun-fuelled spectacle hits its peak. By late morning, the orchard is home to a range of species long extinct, or grown very rare, in Britain. And it would appear that they haven't read the rulebook. Chequered skipper butterflies dance around scabious at the orchard's edge. Large tortoise-shells glide down to take the minerals from an early, young apple that has been knocked off the tree during the night – perhaps by a beech marten. A wryneck makes a brief foray down to an enormous anthill, growing in a fallow area at the back of the farmhouse, before heading off towards its nest; some old woodpecker hole concealed deep in the orchard. The sheer plasticity of nature – its willingness to thrive around and beside us – is truly driven home.

Orchard after orchard, village after village, mile after mile of softly farmed land, the Carpathian village ecosystem is chemically unscathed, varied, small-scale and effortlessly 'scruffy'. But it freestyles on a huge scale; a sympathetic farmland system spanning not kilometres but *countries*. Unlike most of Europe and, increasingly, large parts of the globe, there is no discernible evidence that its insect abundance is yet to fall into serious decline.

As I watch the butterflies thicken on the flowers, as if they are truly under siege, it is hard to imagine here, and now, that the very future of insects on our planet is far from assured. Yet in a chilling 'mega-study' published in 2019, the author Francisco Sanchez-Bayo brought together all scientific evidence of insect decline on our planet, and wrote:

> The conclusion is clear: unless we change our ways of producing food, insects as a whole will go down the path of extinction in a few decades. The repercussions this will have for the planet's ecosystems are catastrophic to say the least, as insects are at the structural and functional base of many of the world's ecosystems since their rise almost 400 million years ago.[1]

Yet sitting in the Carpathian orchard, the solutions to reversing one of the most devastating mass extinctions on our planet seem neither radical nor extreme. The bee-pollinated apples, the hedgehog-gardened vegetables, the pest-removal services of bats and barn owls, are neither difficult to achieve – nor do they preclude a life beside people. Here is a land of apples, pears, timber and honey. As I take it all in, a small herd of cattle have quietly entered the orchard. They, too, will soon contribute to the local village menu. Indeed, in the farmed woodland glades that stretch across the Carpathians, there may genuinely lie the largest thriving insect ecosystem anywhere on Earth where humans *also* live, farm and thrive.

Soon, and at a global scale, it will be the loss of insects, as much as giants, that defines the damage we have done to our own planet – and how poorly we can now harvest the dregs of our once rich home. And yet, in sharing systems such as orchards, we find small solutions that could one day be writ large. If we wish to help reverse the impending extinction of the little lives, then the mass creation of orchards is de facto common sense. And if we can rebuild around us the more self-sustaining landscapes of our past, then we might just arrive at some salvation for our farming in the future.

AUGUST

WHAT LIES BENEATH

BEN

For thee, thou need'st no such deceit,
For thou thyself art thine own bait.

JOHN DONNE

I'm crouched by the brook at the far side of Oak Orchard. Here in another forgotten corner, a fungal stand of alders just about hangs in the soil. Boughs ragged, bored by wood-peckers and beetles, the collective chaos recalls a disturbingly large game of pick-up-sticks. I study the root systems with some degree of self-interest. In spite of their unruly angles, it would seem the alders will rot standing up – and that is exactly how alders are supposed to work.

Alders make perfectly decent living trees. Their catkins are prime bounty for siskins and redpolls; their boughs the home of numerous moths, like the endearingly-named alder kitten. But alders become of greatest use to the natural world as they start to decompose. A 'pioneer' species, alder is often one of the first native British trees to colonise damp soil. On becoming established, it forms a symbiotic relationship unseen by those who stroll past them on a riverside walk. These lofty feathered trees conspire with a bacterium. *Frankia alni* nestles deep in the roots of Britain's common alders. It absorbs nitrogen from the air, making this crucial fertilising element readily accessible to the tree. Alders, in photosynthesising, produce the sugars that the bacterium craves. This apparently insignificant symbiosis means that by decaying in situ, then eventually tumbling into the swampy waters below, an alder leaves behind it additional nitrogen in the soil. It is in the wake of the alder, therefore, that other invaluable riverside trees, like willows, can best take root and thrive.[1]

Much as the alders fascinate me, a decaying rainforest in farmland Britain, I am here on a more primal kind of hunt. Three weeks earlier, Nick's keen eye had detected the paw-prints of an otter in the raw, wet mud at the edge of Clapperley Brook. Otters are rapidly recolonising Herefordshire, and alder roots provide the perfect den site for females; a dense subterranean cave with roots for ceiling beams, from which she and her kits can sally forth each night to hunt fish in clear waters slithery with roach. As the sun sets, I am hoping that at least one member of Herefordshire's burgeoning otter population will finally give itself up. We may have uncovered a lot in this orchard, but like any natural history venture, more forays still end in failure than success. I see not one ripple of an otter.

On closer inspection, the microclimate of the alder swamp dances with pairs of tiny wings. The evening water shimmers with midges, drinking hoverflies and sawflies. The sawflies are the most primitive members of the super-family *Hymanoptera* that contains our bees, wasps and flies. Saw-like genitalia are used to cut through leaves and lay eggs, and several species here at the orchard, like the alder sawflies landing momentarily on the water's static sheen, are clever mimics of hornets. They are one of many smaller orders we have often overlooked in our forays here; most frequently seen in the bills of woodpeckers or flycatchers as they visit their own nests.

But my interest in sawflies is sadly shorter-lived than they are. The screams of summer are upon me. Pitching out of the sultry evening air, around fifty common swifts take me completely by surprise. From several hundred metres overhead, the scimitar flock are now hurtling low over the stream. So fast do swifts feed over water that it's scarcely credible they have caught anything at all – yet each will snatch 20,000 insects in the course of a long day spent entirely in the air.[2] The swifts do not even slow up as they cut through the midge cloud and hurtle on, through the alder swamp, downstream. Swifts generally feed high up in their air, but the low pressure of a gathering August storm has brought them closer to the ground. Across the world, various swift species are seen, rightly, as portents of coming rains. In Sumatra, one, the giant swiftlet, hunts only on the very forefront of enormous storms. From personal experience, the sighting of this bird also signals that within five minutes or less, you will be very wet indeed.

British swifts, outside of a few old-growth pine forests in Scotland, no longer nest in trees – and seeing them appear in the alder swamp seems ecologically nostalgic. This sudden party have come from the orchard's nearest colony at Clapperley Church; a Norman 'stone tree', as the swifts see it, a mile or so upstream. Over the years, I've become so accustomed to seeing swifts over towns that you forget many of their most vital feeding grounds are still rooted in the older ecosystems of our country. In Birmingham and Manchester, for example, whose old indus-trial buildings provide swifts with the perfect nooks to nest, they will still spend much of their time hawking over the old canal networks where, like here, the clear waters and rotting alders conspire to provide fuzzy clouds of insects that keep the swifts well-fed. As my swifts move on, their banshee-like collective shrieks fading into the distance, the first raindrops strike. Soon the still water is fizzing, the midges remorseless, and I call it a night.

In a few days time, the swifts will be gone. Their single brood soon on the wing, we will often see them in screaming parties, whizzing low over the orchard in inclement weather, before their own long journey to the Congo will begin. Now, many orchard birds having fledged their young, they vanish into the verdant hedgerows and impenetrable crowns of oaks. Feeding up, building muscle memory and learning to avoid predations are all activities that take place best under cover of silence. And August is, at first glance, a quiet month for the orchard's wildlife. At first glance.

In the warmth of late summer, the orchard's micro-worlds become the busiest of places. August is a transitory time for many insects, with arrivals and departures on an almost daily basis. In the last year of writing our diary, a welcome nomad invaded the orchard in huge numbers: the painted lady. While many British butterflies are in critical decline, the nomadic lifestyle of the painted lady renders it able to somewhat cheat the odds. It moves through the British landscape like a transient; settling, often in impressive numbers, wherever the last reserves of nectar can be found. Naturalists worldwide are just beginning to realise quite how remarkable the painted lady migration is. Covering 12,000 kilometres, this global butterfly movement is in fact *double* the length of the famed monarch migration of North America.

Painted ladies will often begin their travels in tropical Africa, powering at fifty kilometres an hour over the sand dunes of the Sahara – before entering the Mediterranean. By July and August, generally, the peak of their numbers hits our shores – and in some years, like 2009, up to eleven million butterflies can cross the English Channel. In 2019, the year that the orchard was colonised, painted ladies were even being seen on the island of St Kilda. They may not, even there, have concluded their epic migration. Some butterflies push as far north as the Arctic Circle. Theirs is a life spent entirely on the move.

As a result, painted ladies deposit their eggs in 'waves'. Their migration is neither a marathon nor is it a sprint – it is instead a relay race, with each generation pushing onwards to the north. In July 2019, it was clear that vast numbers were being seen in Cyprus and other Mediterranean islands. By August, the painted wave hit Britain. The numbers in the hop-kiln garden were quite a sight. The Carpathian carpet of butterflies I had travelled overseas to enjoy in July had followed me back home!

Dodging between their ranks, hummingbird hawk-moths had also arrived in good numbers – their wings a blur, shimmering at seventy unseen beats per second; the five-centimetre proboscis flashing in and out of the honeysuckle flowers. There is always something incongruous about hummingbird hawk-moths. It would be easy to laugh that, each year, thousands of the public mistake them for hummingbirds, yet the resemblance is so striking to the casual eye that this seems entirely justified. No other British denizen is so brazen in its mimicry of another animal kingdom. Soon, the painted ladies will continue to push northwards on their epic migration; the hummingbirds head south towards the Mediterranean. August is a time of rapid change. The orchard's many nectar thieves pass one another fleetingly – then go their separate ways.

Now is the time of wasps and wasp mimics; of hornets and leafcutters. In recent years, Nancy has worked hard to establish honeybee colonies in the orchard, but she has also provided five-star accommodation for some of their more solitary relatives. Simple blocks of untreated timber, with deep, narrow bore holes drilled into them, yet stopping short of the back, these bee hotels had always engaged my interest. Now they grabbed my attention. It hadn't been there the week before, but in my absence from the orchard, a perfectly sealed leaf home had been quietly installed!

Few are more ingenious than those who build their homes from leaves. Patchwork leafcutter bees readily go unnoticed, as they can appear similar to honeybees. On closer inspection, you will find that females have a little 'pollen brush', like a yellow, nectar-stuffed Brillo pad, below their abdomens.

The home of a leafcutter bee is as neat as the manner in which its materials are collected. On the adjacent roses growing in the hedge-line of Oak Orchard, sections of waxy leaf cuticle were missing, with edging too precise for any human secateurs. The telltale cutwork of a patchwork leafcutter bee is unmistakable. From each rose leaf, with unfailing regularity, are taken two or three perfect circles of vegetation. The female will then carry these leaf fragments, some longer than she is, below her body – and back to her tubular home. Here, she will use her saliva to stitch the leaves together: a thimble-like quilt of extraordinary finesse. These little leaf homes, like some conjuring act, had now appeared within one of the bee hotel's tiny entrances. I had come late to the party; so rapidly had the female rushed to complete her winter sarcophagus in time.

Female leafcutters know that by the time their eggs hatch, they will be long dead. Entombing a little womb for one who will rise from within it is therefore key to their survival. Once a female's patchwork thimble is constructed, rolled as carefully as the finest cigarillo, females will pack their leafy nesting cells with nectar, pollen and a single egg. The whole chamber is then sealed up to provide a safe place for the young bee to develop: a stuffed vine-leaf, filled with all the ingredients for new life.

Within a single tunnel of the leafcutter bee may often be found five, or even as many as twenty, of these parcelled cells. Once the tunnel's cells have been safely installed, the final masterstroke of co-ordination comes as the female seals shut the chlorophyll sarcophagus. Using her forelegs, she holds the final leaf flush against the entrance of the hole, then uses her saliva to glue the tomb shut. As she hums off into the late summer air, the female will not make it through the winter. In their little rolled homes, her larvae will hatch, feast on the nectar, and then pupate within the sealed space. Spending the cold of winter hibernating as pupae, the following spring the adults burst out through the green sarcophagus door. When they do, they will become one of the orchard's most effective pollinators.

In all my time here, I had entirely overlooked the impossible sight, unless seen at close range, of a leaf migrating unaided through the air. How many times had a leaf surfed quietly over my oblivious head, on course to create nature's most intricate winter survival kit of all? So fast-changing is the seasonality of Britain's wildlife, so myriad its layers, that each year we are caught napping as extraordinary spectacles come and go. Each year, like clumsy intruders, we try, and often fail, to keep up with the relentless rhythms of the orchard.

By mid-August, Maze Orchard, the oldest of the three, has a thriving population of hoverflies. The tiger-patterned marmalade hoverfly, its boggling purple eyes resembling a Pixar animation, is the most familiar. By August, it flies in its thousands. Many are drawn to the apple blossom and act as important pollinators, but in August, in particular, marmalade hoverflies carpet the stands of wild mint at the edges of the hop-kiln gardens. Here, males guard sunny spots by hovering within the most minuscule of sunbeams, holding their position far longer even than a kestrel. The same individual, having chased off a male, then 'whizzes' back to his same spot – and hovers again. The manner of the chase is truly cartoonish, and I am now reminded of an early Disney movie by the way in which the characters in this mint battle zoom – then stop – quivering in mid air.

Perhaps due to the conspicuous defence of their airspace, marmalade hoverflies often appear in the bills of the hop-kiln flycatchers, yet that seems to have little impact on their numbers. While the marmalade hoverfly is a migrant, arriving from the continent in late summer, many of the orchard's hoverflies are born and bred within its boughs. Britain has over 280 species of hoverflies, and new ones are discovered each year. Often, only microscopic examination will discover which is which. The average lifespan of a hoverfly is just twelve days, but the pretty pseudo-wasps that we enjoy in late August are merely the final expression of a far longer life within these trees.

The secret of the orchard hoverflies' success lies not only in the abundant sources of late summer nectar – but in tiny wetlands deep within the apple trees themselves. Here, females will deposit their eggs. Their larvae will develop within the safety of wooden wetland caves. Many of the hoverflies that thrive best in the orchard are, like our colourful death-squad of blue and great tits, consummate carnivores of aphids. Around 40 per cent of Britain's hoverflies specialise in aphids, and this renders these insects of enormous importance to the health of the orchard – and its crop.

Female hoverflies of many species will seek out aphid colonies and lay their eggs among them. Hatching amid their future dinner, hoverfly larvae are blind. They make for sinister viewing at first glance, possessing neither obvious legs – nor a head. Instead, the larvae use chemical cues, and touch, to work out where their meal is. The death of the aphid is neither quick nor pleasant. The hoverfly larva locks onto the aphid with glutinous saliva. It pierces the aphid's skin with its long, sharp mouth-hooks – then sucks out its insides. It's a death that even gardeners might hesitate to inflict on one of Britain's most acknowledged agricultural pests. Aphids unfortunate to be consumed by a young larva, in its first instar stage, can expect an even slower demise – lasting several hours. As the hoverfly larva grows, dwarfing the aphids like a giant green growth, it will consume them within minutes.

Given the thousands of hoverflies on the wing each August, their presence will dramatically reduce the numbers of aphids in the orchard as surely as the blue and great tits found nesting in every other tree. Farming without pesticides for decades, Nancy and David have never even considered aphids to be a threat – and few traces of their damage can be found among the orchard trees. While it may serve big business to peddle toxic chemicals to steri-lise an orchard and its crop, in a system as balanced as this one, self-regulation works at every level. Aphids are deci-mated here each year without a chemical in sight – often, by the enemy *within*.

But the orchard's hoverflies do not get it all their own way. One year, I was rooting around at the orchard edge, searching for a late chiffchaff's nest, when I discovered something truly macabre. At the top of one flowering cluster of white-petalled daisies, I found no fewer than three hover-flies. Petrified in death, each was dusted in a soft white coating; a garden of white hairs growing from the abdomen. Each of their wings were still eerily outstretched in one, never-ending flight – as if the sinister force that had taken them were still mocking them long after their demise. This silent cemetery led to the discovery of a story that is, quite literally, mind-blowing.

What few people know is that the orchards and mead-owlands of Britain play host to a zombie phenomenon as sinister as any of the tropical rainforest.[3] Here, in early autumn, a fungus, *Entomophthora*, becomes the scourge of the orchard's hoverflies. Its spores carry low in the air – and are unwittingly swallowed by the flies as they search for nectar. Scientists believe that *Entomophthora* prefers its hosts to be cool.[4] So the waning days of August, with its falling evening temperatures, coupled with the orchard's abundance of late summer hoverflies, provide the perfect time for the fungus to strike.

Over its incubation period within the fly, which can last between five and eight days, the fungal spore will slowly take control of the hoverfly's airborne body. Once inhaled, the fungus's germ-tube expands into a bladder-like alien body, which then scatters further hyphae, or fungal tubes, throughout the hapless hoverfly – still, at this point, flying in the air. Most of these fungi invade the fat, then the tissues, of its abdomen. This process will eventually kill the hoverfly, but first, *Entomophthora* must decide where the hoverfly is to die. Now, *Entomophthora* begins to control the hoverfly's *mind*.

The hoverflies are 'steered', against what free will they have left, to land on the very tops of flowering plants. This gives *Entomophthora* spores the greatest chance of being wind-borne for longer distances – after the hoverfly has died. Before its demise, the hoverfly is made to perform one final act. It is forced to spread its wings – and clamp its furrowed feet to the flower. Locked here in a dying embrace, the hoverfly appears, for one final time, to 'hover': a sinister nod to its former living self. Then, the fungus explodes from its body. Leaving the hoverfly a white garden of fungal tubes, the spores of *Entomophthora* now carry on the wind. Soon, they will drift down the throats of the hoverflies around – oblivious that they, too, will soon become the next generation of orchard zombies. So successful is *Entomophthora* that, under the cooler conditions of late summer, over 90 per cent of infected flies will succumb to a fate worse than death.

Unlike some of the orchard's symbiotic relationships, the relationship of the hoverfly to its fungus could be described as distinctly one-sided. Yet even this is another form of natural regulation. *Entomophthora* may not be the most appealing denizen of this orchard – but it serves an invaluable function. By controlling hoverflies and a range of other species, *Entomophthora* prevents the population of any one species from growing out of control. Were, for example, all the orchard's hoverflies to remain intact, hunted only by a few specialist birds such as spotted flycatchers, their numbers too would grow to plague proportions. Aphid numbers would drastically fall – to such low levels, perhaps, that even blue tits would struggle to find food. So these little death gardens of fungal zombies, therefore, turn out to be just another means by which the orchard regulates and balances itself.

During the latter half of August, the hedgerows and margins of the orchard become brightly-coloured sugar-magnets. Among the most desirable, and not only for the fruit-pickers on the orchard's single public footpath, is the deep purple 'frogspawn' of the elderberry. As with so many other species, our relationship with elder trees has changed over the years. The Anglo-Saxons considered elder sacred. The Hylde Moer, or Elder Mother, was a spirit deemed resident within the tree. The Hylde Moer's power was to turn the tree's recognised bounty – of flowers, berries and wood – into blessings.[5] If an elder grew near a dwelling, it was deemed a protective force. It would be easy to dismiss these Germanic gestures of respect, yet these people were more observant than many of us today. Now, elder is grubbed by local councils, by many conservationists, and from our gardens; part of the much-maligned 'scrub' that in fact constitutes one of our richest natural habitats. Many modern ecologists or gardeners might have something to learn from our Anglo-Saxon ancestors.

Ecologically, elder retains huge importance throughout the year. In the breeding season, its soft bark crawls with micromoths, making it a beloved tree for small insectivores. The orchard's hedgerow-nesting marsh tits can also be found taking elder berries in family groups, uttering their sharp sneeze calls as they are chased off by the squadrons of blackbirds and mistle thrushes who dominate this real estate. The orchard's old hedgerows and undrained ditches provide a safe refuge for elder – and as August pushes into September, its berries become yet another crucial lifeline in the relentless march of the orchard's seasonal year.

The blackberries are ripening – and species scramble to adapt. The orchard's plentiful common wasps now renounce their habitual carnivory in favour of a sucrose snack. During early summer, the life of our wasps has been cooperative, regimented, disciplined: intense. Wasp nests up to five thousand strong, packed into the orchard's cavities, root systems and abandoned bank vole holes, result in adults frothing out from the familiar paper sculptures started by the colony queen in the spring. Known to increasingly fewer of us from our garden sheds, this wood-pulp latticed metropolis contains row upon ordered row of egg cells. From each, in which the queen has laid an egg, female workers hatch –

and fan out across the orchard in search of prey. If the queen is the layer and the leader, these workers are the assassins. This far-roaming kill squad must be among the most deadly yet seen in the orchard. Across Britain in a summer, worker wasps, in the course of feeding the larvae in each cell of the queen's nest, are estimated to consume fourteen million kilograms of invertebrate prey[6] – the weight of twenty thousand bull elephants.

As a constant stream of caterpillars, spiders, other flies and even butterflies – all chemically petrified by their wasp predators – are carried back into the wasps' nest, their larvae swell rapidly. Hatching into fertile males and unmated princesses, most wasps in the orchard will leave the nest come July. Then, as August mellows, the orchard's wasps undergo a change of character. No longer needing to feed their young in the nest, thousands of workers now disperse through the orchard, bereft of caterpillar-killing purpose. More and more of their prey is approaching hibernation. Now, wasps exchange the life of hunter-gatherers for a seat at the orchard's most bankable dining table. They descend upon apples, not even waiting for them to fall – and onto the blackberries that flank the orchard's every wall.

No longer needing the protein to grow their larvae, the orchard's wasps choose instead the sugars that, converted into carbohydrates by their fast metabolisms, will increase their chances of making it through the winter. As summer fades, wasps may become increasingly bad-tempered, as the alcohol of over-ripe plums ferments in their guts, causing fights to break out – and unwary humans, on occasion, to be stung.

The switch of wasps from insect prey to sugary fruit marks, for us, the end of the orchard summer. Now, the avian breeding cycles of all but sex-crazed woodpigeons is drawn to an elegant close. Skeletal blue tit parents – colours and fat reserves fading – raid the hedgerows for small moths, aphids and berries. For the next six months, the seasonal supermarket of the countryside will close. As August fades, every sugar flaunts its wares.

As September beckons, gone is the buzzing air. The fruits of autumn hang heavy in the trees. A strange lull breaks the relentless pace of the fruiting forest. After the struggles and chaos of the breeding months, nature gently relaxes her shoulders – and takes stock.

SEPTEMBER

FLY BY NIGHTS

NICK

When spider webs unite, they can tie down a lion.

AFRICAN PROVERB

Giant winged insects stream from the ground, glowing and silhouetted in the bright moonlight. Six gangly legs trail below each airborne craft. A close-up look at their faces reveals bulging, over-sized eyes, scanning as they search for their quarry. Tales of these being Britain's most poisonous animal flash through my mind. And most alarmingly, every so often a mutant would fly past, a head at each end, two sets of wings flitting furiously and a body conjoined in the middle.

Lying among the damp meadow grass of Hop Kiln Orchard, my head-torch drawing arcs about me in the night air, I had chanced upon an ephemeral autumn spectacle.

For nearly a year, young cranefly larvae – leatherjackets – have been busily chomping their way through grass roots. Pupating in July, they have been waiting for this night, a perfect blend of conditions that trigger a mass-hatching event. Just a month ago, the ground here was parched: cracked and brittle after another dry August. But a brief afternoon thunderstorm, following a week of sporadic showers, has left the grass lush; the soil, expectant and moist.

Wriggling themselves a small gap in their earthen cocoons and orienting themselves vertically, cranefly chrysalises split open down the length of their heads, as the adults push themselves upwards to freedom. Somehow, across the orchard, all the leatherjackets seem to know that tonight is *the* night – apparently communicating via some subliminal social network in the soil and agreeing the time and date for this extravagant, synchronised party. By flooding the prey market like this, craneflies ensure that despite the efforts of the orchard's most agile bats, and the predators that await them as the sun comes up, huge numbers will survive to produce the next generation.

As I watch, more and more hordes pour forth from the ground. That solid soil can give way to tens of thousands of winged insects is still hard to comprehend. Female craneflies hatch with mature eggs and can mate as soon as they are out of the soil. Males patrol the night air, hawking for any signs of a mate. Timing is everything. Every so often, *balls* of craneflies pile on top of each other, almost crawling their way back into the ground as they try to be the one to bind with a freshly emerging female. Watching from less than a metre away, I can *hear* the noises they make, as dozens of wings clatter against each other, oblivious to anything that isn't a member of the opposite sex. Some craneflies literally lose limbs in the frenzy, as dew-toothed grass blades interrupt this insatiable drive to mate, gripping onto their legs with surface tension that turns them into Venus fly traps. Whoever wins this search emerges twice the size from this writhing, fragile sea. Tails lock together, in a mating embrace that can last for hours. As the losers disperse, just the odd forgotten leg lies twitching on the ground.

Growing up, craneflies were a species that yielded much intrigue to a young naturalist. When these creatures appeared each autumn around the school playground, hushed whispers went around that they were 'so poisonous that if you ate one, it could kill you', the only problem being that they didn't 'have the mouthparts to inject their lethal venom'. But it got worse, as each year, people sleeping would 'accidentally swallow them and never wake up!'. The colloquially named daddy longlegs was a beast to be revered and respected. Under no circumstances should it be touched. Just in case.

All of this is an urban myth – yet one that persists remarkably well when you mention daddy longlegs to anyone. The only basis in fact is that indeed they don't have mouthparts of any use. Once flying, craneflies don't feed; instead living off the energy reserves they built up as larvae. Most craneflies that bumble their way into rooms, and persistently clatter into street lights at this time of year, are all of the same species – the European cranefly.

Nonetheless, craneflies *do* deserve to be revered and respected. They form a crucial food source for our wildlife, at every stage of their strange lives.

Leatherjackets – cranefly larvae – are one of the main food sources for breeding wading birds, such as curlews and redshank. The last few lapwings that we see trying to nest in the nearby fields rely on the leatherjackets found in unsprayed pasture and grassland for their chicks. In the orchard, the feeding forays of our few valuable pairs of starlings consist of frequent probing searches for leather-jackets: young starlings grow up on a diet of little else. Crows, magpies and rooks can be seen across the summer probing the soil looking for these fat nutritious grubs, while the orchard's healthy mole population shuffle around their underground networks on the hunt for any that drop into their feeding tunnels.

While thousands of craneflies succumb to predators as larvae here in the orchard, their emergence as adults is equally important, fuelling the swallows and redstarts for their southerly migrations, at the same time giving the orchard's bats an autumnal feast. But only organic woodland pastures yield such extraordinary numbers of craneflies. Across Britain, this vital annual emergence – unseen under the cover of darkness – is slowly disappearing. Glyphosate, the world's most 'popular' weedkiller, is the most widely used agricultural herbicide in our country: applied across 5.4 million acres of British farmland – 23 per cent of the total agricultural area.[1] Gardeners are still heavily encour-aged to use it – presented with lurid-coloured bottles on supermarket shelves, promising the delicious prospect of insect oblivion. The impact of this one chemical on our soil invertebrates is not just eye-watering: it's damning.

The Soil Association has looked at every stage of earthworm lifecycles, including reproductive success, juvenile growth and feeding ability. All are reduced when earthworms are exposed to glyphosate. The most urgent statistic was that the hatching success of earthworm cocoons reduced by between 55 and 60 per cent, when exposed to glyphosate.[2] If any chemical was known to reduce a vertebrate's breeding success or impacted human health in this way, it would be banned overnight.

Out of sight below ground, this cancer of the soil is turning diverse subterranean jungles into silent deserts. Healthy soils are as important for our countryside as a healthy gut is for ourselves. They turn by-products and waste into available nutrients, minerals and organic products. Glyphosate, however, inhibits the microbial world hidden within the soil. When this digestive reactor is imbalanced, the effects are far reaching. While the most detailed studies so far apply to earthworms, studies in countries like the Netherlands are uncovering that other invertebrates with a comparable ecology – leatherjackets very much included – are suffering a similar fate.

This enormous loss of soil invertebrate biomass doesn't just interrupt the food chain for the creatures that feed on them. Just a few miles from this orchard, farmers and gardeners alike are soaking chemicals into the land across the year; killing the soil they rely on at an unfathomable rate. Only chemical-free grassland management – exactly that seen beneath these orchard trees – allows a rich soil biodiversity to thrive, ensuring spectacles such as the incredible synchronised cranefly emergence return year after year.

Guided by weak moonlight, I follow the fresh craneflies as they clumsily bounce off anything and everything, accompanied by the sound of autumnal apple leaves and decaying grass-seed stalks whispering in the light night breeze. Winding over to Maze Orchard, the torchlight now picks out silvery, reflective lines hanging delicately between the meadow fronds. Under each of these master lines – bending under the night's dew – hides another of the orchard's master predators.

From funnels to tunnels, horizontal carpets to vertical trellises, glue-filled guide ropes to fishing nets, September is the month to enjoy our country's outstanding diversity of arachnid architects. Sweeping a torch beam through any vegetation on a cold misty evening reveals just how busy spiders are, as the orchard's grassland margins transform into a tangled and shimmering world, painted with strands of glistening silk.

Spaced through the orchard, often around the base of a fallen tree, Nancy and David have let free-standing clumps of bramble transform into thorn-studded igloos. Over the years, these self-willed blackberry bushes have provided safe refuge to nests of wrens and long-tailed tits, dunnocks and blackbirds. Now, silent of song or punky thrush broods, these orchard fortresses appear empty. But new nurseries are quietly growing here among the hostile barbs.

With the precision of a tiny mechanical robot, a female walnut orb weaver, picked out in the torchlight, is caught in the act of building her new home. Moored between an apple trunk one side and a ragwort stalk the other, she floats in mid-air; clinging on to the wires of her new fly swat. By day, she'll sit hidden in a recess in the bark, a single signalling thread keeping her aware of anything that touches her trap. But now, the walnut orb spider brazenly waits out in the open, poised at the centre of her silken telephone; eight legs listening – alert. Her abdomen is stencilled with the ribbed pattern of a perfectly symmetrical oak leaf. Two prominent dimples are the anchor points for powerful internal muscles. These allow her to flat-pack herself into tiny crevices; an auto-dismantling IKEA kit.

Despite having carefully woven a new web, she is not interested in catching any of the orchard's nocturnal fliers this evening. Having laced her pheromonal perfume around her web, she retires to the middle, and waits. Sporting a swollen abdomen, she is only interested in one thing.

Like most orb weavers, and indeed most spiders, walnut orb spider males are a lot smaller than females. But what he may lack in size, the male certainly makes up for in swagger. To attract a lady, male walnut orb weavers strut their stuff with some impressive dance moves. His routine starts with percussion; raising both front legs in the air and frenetically drumming her web to signal his arrival. Often performed under cover of darkness, his dance can be entirely judged via the medium of vibration. If she responds favourably – spider talk for she hasn't *yet* eaten him – he'll test his luck further.

Edging towards his prospective mate, the male begins his dance routine; trying to impress her with a variety of taps and shakes, sneaking forward with each step. By freezing, she signals her approval for this approach, remaining motionless as he uses his front two feet to tickle her head and thorax; the ultimate flirtatious advance for a frisky spider. Our now cavalier male makes his move, flitting underneath the female and injecting her with one of his pedipalps – the large club-like sperm-storing organs that sit at the front of his face – before attempting a quick getaway. This is the only cue the female needs in the whole routine. Her eggs now fertilised, she has only one use for her now previous boyfriend. As he tiptoe-retreats out of her nest, she lunges. Eating the male will feed her developing eggs. Yet even as he dies, the male ensures that while distracted by eating *him*, she won't be able to mate with any of his rivals.

Old walls are wonderful habitats. Shaped by the elements, their crumbling cavities, mortar cracks and coarse bricks provide homes for all orders of life. It's easy to discard their autumnal importance, long after the flycatcher chicks have left their little nooks – but by night, these rock faces come alive; crawling with armoured woodlice and bright orange centipedes, tiny mites and octopedal harvestmen.

A finely woven lattice gently ripples as my breath gifts it a light breeze. It's a subtle plate of silk, surrounded by a dozen fine tripwires that radiate towards its centre: a tiny monochrome dartboard. At its bulls-eye is a penny-sized opening; a tapering black hole, plaited into a small recess in the mortar. Peering in, the void appears empty. No one at home? Plucking a strand of grass, I tickle the edge of this flat web, catching one of the trip-wires. The subtle vibration draws a subtle reaction: a single black leg nudges from the void, resting on the rim of its satellite dish. A second tickle induces a second leg – both now poised, 'listening' for more information via tiny spider foot hairs. Spiders are able to use such signals to triangulate *what* might have landed on their web – and how far from the entrance it is. A third tickle results in the reaction I hoped for, as an adult female tube web spider lunges out of the hole and clamps onto the grass, attempting to drag her spoils back to safety.

This strange orchard resident is a green-fanged tube web spider – named after the iridescent sheen that her jaws reflect in the moonlight. A consummate recluse, her character changes completely when food crosses her path, fearlessly tackling prey far larger than herself with a pair of sharp fangs on the end of bulbous jaws. Like two needles, these jaws easily pierce through the exoskeletons of her insect prey, delivering a cocktail of protein neurotoxins[3] that induce quick paralysis. Nocturnal caterpillars stand no chance, while even large moths are rapidly incapacitated before being dragged back into the dark safety of her cavity. Fortunately for me, her bite is no danger to humans.[4]

The tube web spider's fierce territoriality is well directed. Hidden inside her funnel, protected by a wall of stone behind and the shining green weapons of their well-armed mother in front, are her babies. Encased in a hollow silk chamber, they have just hatched. With the first frosts less than a month away, they must rapidly gain weight before dispersing to find their own winter caverns. With the clock ticking, it is time for this mother to make the ultimate sacrifice.

Remarkably, the female green-fanged tube web spider will raise a family and then die within her own mortar tomb, allowing her babies to fatten up on her own body before they leave home. By recycling the nutrients she sequesters in her own body and handing these down to her offspring, she ensures they will have the energy reserves needed to hibernate through the toughest of winters. And there is a fair chance that when we check this cavity in the spring, one of the green-fang mother's offspring will have adopted this very same spot. Fattened on the bodies of caterpillars and moths, who themselves fed on these trees, the orchard's nutrients continue to flow, recycle and rejuvenate life – through the very smallest of food webs.

Wandering among the old apples on an unseasonably warm September evening in the middle of the month, I switch off the head-torch and allow my senses to adjust to the dwindling glow of a waxing moon. In the stillness, even the sound of my own breathing rattles this quiet landscape. Yet all around howls a tornado of noise. Shrills, trills, screeches and screams cut through the air – an energetic chorus of bad singing. The blessing is, *my* ears can't hear them.

In German the singers are 'flitter mice'. In Gaelic they are known as 'leather wings'. In Catalan they translate, rather unflatteringly, as the 'rats that make clumps'.[5] The original derivation of their English name is 'flapper', though by the late sixteenth century they'd been upgraded to 'rattle-mice'. Despite receiving a mixed reception across history, bats today seem to be far better received – and the Malverns, with its profusion of veteran trees, nocturnal flying snacks and old-growth buildings, is one of the most important bat refuges left in our country.

While humans assimilate visual light cues, transmitted via our eyes, to build a view of our planet's riches, bats see using their *ears*. By firing out a steady pulse of ultra-high-pitched clicks, then listening to how quickly these bounce back to them from their surroundings, bats are able to navigate in the pitch black. This process happens thousands of times every second, giving the bats a continually morphing reality – the equivalent of us being able to see just ten metres in front of us at a time yet the view rebuilding every time we blink. Some bats, like the large ginger-coated noctules, shout so loudly that if we could hear one, it would be four times the legal volume limit of a nightclub.[6] The louder bats shout, the further they can see.

Fortunately, if you're a bat, the orchard is stuffed with a rich flying banquet. Moths and beetles, mayflies and lacewings, winged ants and craneflies, mosquitoes and gnats, all provide a wide choice of seasonal produce on this airborne menu. Throughout the summer, our bats feast, using every trick in the book to ensure they outsmart a potential dinner. One of the cleverest tactics is that recently discovered in a real ancient woodland specialist – the barbastelle. While bats are emitting their calls, some moth species have learned to dial in to these and use them as a warning signal to help avoid predation. But barbastelles are the stealth fighter jets of the bat world. They've altered their call routine, so that the closer they fly to their prey, the quieter their calls become.[7] As the barbastelles zero in on their target, their sound signature implies they are flying away. Once the moth finally hears the approaching bat, it's too late.

While avoiding trees and stealthily finding food are important, there is another purpose to the shrieks made by bats. Come late summer, having fattened up on choice orchard morsels, male noctule bats go house-hunting. Whirring between the orchard trees, they are prospecting for a special type of cavity: the perfect bachelor pad. Fortunately, the orchard's cabinet-makers often abandon their old projects, leaving carefully crafted and well-insulated homes free to the most persistent of bidders. Old woodpecker holes are the ideal stage from which male noctules can woo the ladies with a very special performance.

On mild September evenings, these eligible bachelors crawl to the entrances of their newfound homes – and begin to sing. From a scoresheet of clicks, purrs and buzzes, they recite a repertoire that is irresistible to passing females. The most successful serenades result in the visitation of over a dozen female noctules[8] – all squeezing in to the male's rustic love shack for a brief two-day courtship. By early October, the male noctule's most important work of the year will be complete. With the first frosts imminent, he returns to piling on the final few grams needed to get through hibernation, a period in which he might go without food for up to four long, cold months. Even for the largest British bat, abundant autumnal insects, allowing for plentiful fat deposits, are the difference between life and death ahead of a harsh winter.

Earlier in the summer, David had let us know of a spectacle that had been setting off his security cameras. Each morning, just before dawn, his whole yard would *fill* with bats. We were intrigued – and even more so after seeing some video of it. But watching the infra-red recording back on a small monitor felt like watching the Last Night of the Proms on an aeroplane screen. Without sound. This was clearly an event that was best enjoyed live. Tickets were freely available. They just demanded a *very* early start.

And that is how Ben and I found ourselves driving up to Herefordshire at 3.30 a.m. on a late July morning, hoping to experience this for ourselves. Wrapped in too many clothes and armed with bat detectors and a thermos of coffee, we quietly walked into the middle of the courtyard and sat down. Not quite sure what to expect, the bat detector kept us awake, by periodically reminding us that the odd common pipistrelle was hawking overhead. Pipistrelles are our smallest bat species; so tiny they can fit inside a matchbox. But their stature doesn't reduce their appetites, as these ravenous insect-hoovers can demolish over three thousand mosquitoes each night. As the clock edged closer to dawn, we increasingly wondered if we'd chosen the wrong spot; there were a few bats here, but nothing like the numbers that David had showed us. Perhaps we'd missed it for the season?

But then, something magical happened. As if from nowhere, bats began to appear, whirring around above our heads. A few pipistrelles turned into a dozen, and the dozens turned into hundreds, their calls so overlaid that the bat detector could only output a frenzied white noise. It was like being on set for the digital render of the Batman movie, as more and more bats were painted in, joining the fervent whirlwind circling around us.

As yet – beyond the fact that it mainly takes place around maternity roosts – no one is exactly sure just why pipistrelles swarm like this at dawn. But after ten minutes, as with the collective decision-making seen in social insects, the gust of pipistrelles decided the show was complete. One by one, they disappeared into the narrowest of openings above the old cider-making barn. Seeing, hearing and feeling a thousand pound-coin-weight pipistrelles swarming around your head before flooding back into the tiniest of gaps, embodies the natural riches still to be found in the last of our traditional orchards. Cartwheeling around each other, the bats' collective energy is the product of the health of this whole ecosystem: a natural endorsement that this is an excellent place to live.

Such biodiversity works best where habitats overlap. Habitats, after all, are just categories – created by ourselves. The species we have assigned to them, however, often need many different habitats to survive. Of all the indicators of a thriving mosaic environment, bats are perhaps the most important. From the deadwood that a Leisler's chooses to roost in, to the open water that a Daubenton's needs to feed over, to the abundant nocturnal beetles favoured by our noctules – the presence of different bat species is a real-time assessment of habitat quality. On any given night throughout spring, summer and autumn, you'll find more species of bats over the orchard here than in many legally-protected forests or nature reserves. There are more species of moth and beetle here than on almost any other kind of modern farm. Some of our rarest bats, including lesser horseshoes and Bechstein's bats, still hunt commonly over the orchard's open lands. No fewer than nine regular species have been recorded flying through the old apples – or hawking for insects around the verdant ivy, wisteria and garden flowers of the hop-kiln garden. Their numerous presence alone affirms that the food chains of the orchard are balanced and working. That, for another year, the orchard has passed its productivity MOT.

As the bats crawl to bed and the sun rises, the autumn orchard sings a different tune. The fuzz of cranefly wings and the delicate rattle of apple leaves has been replaced by a chorus of chatter, emanating from the orchard's profusion of teasels and thistles. A charm of goldfinches are busily working their way through the dried flowerheads. The Anglo-Saxons knew these golden-winged songsters as *thisteltuige* – 'the thistle-tweaker'; an apt name for a bird expert at prising out tiny but protein-rich seeds. Each seed is cracked, bisected, husked and sorted in a few deft beak tweaks, before the bird returns to carefully prising out its next miniature meal. The seeds of these plants are minute, yet goldfinches are able to feed on over ten a minute and so make their energy investment worthwhile.

Among the energetic finches, the warm early light catches the last of the ragwort flowers, turning their bright yellow a rich orange. Still flowering throughout September, their steady supply of nectar and pollen is essential for bumblebee princesses stocking up on their final food shops before hibernation. Nestled between them, the decaying fronds of burdock, wild carrot and dock are now spider sanctums – providing the much-needed altitude required for these silk-painters to hang their work. Even as the meadow appears to die for another autumn, this floral mausoleum remains filled with faunal diversity.

The orchard is now starting to change daily. Covered in their green and red jewels, the apple trees begin to express their own characters: one day decadently clad in colour; the next, having dropped the majority of their precious cargo to the floor. Different colours and shapes combine to create a still-life catwalk: each tree lines up to offer a different take on the fashion of the imminent harvest.

By the end of September, orchard life is beginning to slow down. The trees exhale under the weight of fruit, preparing their leaves for the annual moult. The orchard is about to undergo yet another of its shape-shifting transformations, drawing in a new cast of characters primed to exploit the autumn's riches. But before that, there is work to be done. Walking back towards the car, I hear a gentle thud landing in the wet grass. The apples have decided they are ready to be eaten. Now it is a matter of who gets there first.

OCTOBER

HARVEST

BEN

And sometimes like a gleaner thou dost keep
Steady thy laden head across a brook;
Or by a cyder-press, with patient look,
Thou watchest the last oozings hours by hours.

JOHN KEATS

For the bemused jackdaws perched on the hop-kiln beams, it must be a confusing sight. The cider mill is slowly turning. But as it rotates round and around, it's no longer being pulled by the cider-house donkey of yore. The creature that turns the wheel looks sad and lost. In its past life, one senses, things were a great deal more exciting. It once moved a lot faster. It roamed free across the Herefordshire countryside. It is hard not to feel for its plight, especially as the creature turning the cider mill wheel, trapped in perpetual slow motion, is an old Matchless motorbike, last seen stampeding through the Malverns' lanes in 1961.

The onset of October heralds the frenzied onset of perry-making, as the orchard's consistent crop of pears are quickly swept from below the trees – and brought to the cider mill for crushing. Right now, the mechanical donkey is busy churning pears. Unlike apples, pears must be collected within no more than two days, ideally one, of hitting the ground. With a mental map of his thirty pear trees, David's pace of life is as relentless as the fieldfares swarming through the orchard, as, each dawn, he forages for the latest windfall beside his winged peers.

Inside the old cider house, the still musky air bends under the scent wave of crushed fruit; heavy, rich, warmly inviting. Jackdaws gossip in the beams overhead as David shows me around the old cider mill. We now inspect the mechanical donkey in more detail. This home-spun mill was developed by David's grandfather, Philip. The motorbike's petrol motor has been excised; in its place, an electric motor has been fitted. This drives a series of chains and belts via the bike's front wheel, running in turn to a sprocket in the original gearbox and then to the back wheel. This, in turn, provides the right amount of torque, and wheel speed, needed for the mechanical donkey to be driven in reverse, turning the stone mill wheel – and crushing and milling the thick carpet of Thorn pears in the trough.

They say that no two orchards are the same – and I have never seen this system in action before. As David and I watch the cider mill going about its business, it's clear that this is also a very effective operation, ably spewing out pulped pears. From here, the mush is transferred to the cavernous cider press, calibrated to extract every last drop of amber fuel from the pulp. As the titanic force of a wooden beam squeezes down the mountains of fruit within, the already soft, rain-battered pears are crushed to the consistency of porridge. Between each layer of fruit lies hessian cloth, sometimes, slatted wooden racks will be used instead. Gradually, a fine pear porridge accumulates in the large wooden vessels below.

Eighty per cent of a pear is soluble in the form of juice. Out pours the raw elixir that will create David's unique blend of organic Herefordshire perry. After each batch of milling, the unwanted by-product of this process is dealt with in a rather ingenious fashion. As we leave the hop kiln, the strange sight of condensed orange 'cakes' catches my eye. 'Ah, the Leaning Tower of Pommice.' This, David explains, is his hornet and wasp distraction facility. Here, some way from the main cider-making operation, these amber bricks are the residue of the milling and pressing; the fibrous by-products of the pear, crushed and compressed. We watch from a slight distance as a woozy hornet and several wasps bumble around, land and begin to take their fill. It's another of the orchard's elegant sharing arrange-ments. These towers of tannic offal ensure the orchard's invaluable wasp pollinators fuel up before their winter hibernation; fattening them for their long cold slumber in the coming months. They also ensure the wasps do not feel tempted to enter the buildings where the cider is made.

Like anything in cider-making, there are strong opinions

among traditional cider manufacturers as to what should happen after the pear porridge has been made. 'It depends on the tannic qualities of the pear,' David explains. 'If your pears are very high in tannins, the perry can be extremely dry, so you may want to leave the milled pears to oxidise for some days.' Once the milling, pressing and oxidation process is complete, the pear porridge, the product of the mechanical donkey's hard labour, finally gets to travel across to the adjacent barn.

As we walk towards the cider barn, stopping to inspect the black sheet of droppings below the pipistrelle's maternity roost, the interior of the cider-making unit packs a sudden jolt of crisp modernity. After the musty dank of the hop kiln, there is nothing ancient about David's cider-making barn. The whole unit shines – a blend of plastics and polished metals: sanitised and safe to the highest standards of modern food hygiene. Here is where pear porridge will undergo its transformation into perry. From the new cider press emanates a wave of bitter and sweet as if the ore of crushed fruit is, itself, ablaze; its smoke permeating our clothes. The retrophiliac in me momentarily recoils. This is the first sign of industrial modernity I have seen in years visiting the orchard. Yet this sanitised space is also the key to the orchard's future. Here in the cider barn, the past and future meet. Outside lies a farmed wild wood; a place where nature regulates and rules. Inside shines commerce; the organic cider and perry a source of revenue that will buy December's next batch of new stock and keep the orchard viable in the years to come.

Frothing amber glass jars burst with the promise of winter

fermentation. The darker one, David tells me, is the cherished elixir of the Betty Prosser pear. It already looks ripe and delicious in its sealed glass jar. The large volume of paler brew comes from David's banker for perry: the orchard's Thorn pears. In among them, silently bubbling and stirring, lies a sparkling Moorcroft, produced using the champagne method. Already, as this pear ferments within its jar, carbon dioxide is starting to add the natural 'fizz'.

I watch as the next batch of pear porridge now enters one of the wood-sided fruit presses in the barn. Turning the cider press handle, David exerts one final wrench as the last drop of another Betty Prosser falls. The container is taken to the half-full jar and poured in – and for today, at least, David's work here is done.

So far, it has been a good yield for pears. The hours of sun a pear receives, the volume of rainfall, the strength of early winds and, crucially, the volume of pollinators on the wing, all determine the quality and quantity of the perry crop in a season. Pears here are more consistent performers than some of the apples, which generally have two good years in every four. The windfall at the start of October has been swift and sudden. The ground lies thick. We emerge out of the shiny cider barn into the swirling leaves, mud and chaos of the world we both, instinctively, prefer to inhabit. David walks out into Hop Kiln Orchard, to assess what is left on the ground.

Even as the orchard's custodian, frugivorous surprise is still commonplace for David. His veteran Barland, the 150-year-old split catapult, surviving against all the odds in Maze Orchard, is, David tells me, a Bosbury pear. This is one of the earliest cultivars of perry pears in Herefordshire, going back, as far as is known, to 1650. Its fruits were believed to carry medicinal properties and it is thought to have originated less than ten kilometres to the west in Bosbury, still home to a large assembly of commercial orchards. Walking into Hop Kiln Orchard, David stops at another, its furrowed, leathered skin catching the late winter sun. It's the Betty Prosser. 'Even in the perry-growing heydays, this breed was always rare. We still know very little about it.'

While there will be a few further windfalls of pears, the apples are just starting to thicken the ground. It comes as a surprise to me that cider apples are not collected right away. An old Herefordshire saying is that you must 'leave them to sweat'. If a visible bruise can be seen with gentle pressure of the thumb, then the apple is ready to be picked from the ground. David is a stickler for quality. He assesses each apple before he picks it up. As we inspect the latest fall, most are in excellent condition, the result of the orchard's pest-removal services. It is striking as we pick apple after apple from the ground how rot is absent from the vast majority of the fruit.

'Some years ago,' David explains, 'the representative of a large commercial cider-making firm visited the orchard. On seeing the fruit, he was incredulous that we weren't using a single chemical. We explained the sheer number of insect carnivores in the orchard and he was amazed. Eventually, he found two trees with a tiny bit of leaf curl. That was it.'

We stop below the veteran Kingston Black. Bred in

Somerset, this is one of few remaining trees of the original stock. Its apples are small, blood-red, dark, though not 'black'; this was the name given to them by Somerset fruit-growers centuries before. The tree is still particularly thick with fruit; growing in clusters so dense they look more like giant rowan berries. 'Over time, a lot of these Kingstons have been "improved" to increase the size and yield of the fruit, but then, their rootstock suffers. This is an old standard – it's designed to stand the test of time,' David explains.

We continue our journey through the fruit forest and back towards the hop kiln, scattering winter thrushes and grumpy, drunken wasps. Cider-making, David says, is an acquired art. While commercial orchards have sought to standardise the process, David has no interest in churning out more of the same. His perry is unique – and gets better every year.

In the early days, some noteworthy lessons had been learned. 'One of the worst lessons learned was not to add too high a volume of Red Pear to perry,' he laments. 'It creates a powerful laxative effect – something we weren't keen to repeat in a hurry.' Adding excess sugar to an already strong, fermented brew once created a knock-out cider of over 10 per cent. 'It was incredibly fizzy: no one would go near it.' One setback that is beyond David's control is the weather. Two years ago, October saw an unseasonably warm spell. As temperatures soared to 20 degrees Celsius, the perry's yeasts sprang into hyperdrive – and the whole batch fermented in six days. 'That was an exceptional year – and not a good one,' David reflects. 'For centuries, cider-makers have relied on the cool, stable temperatures of late autumn and winter. A heatwave in October produced a fast-fermented yield that was virtually undrinkable.'

In spite of these setbacks in his early days as a cider-maker, David is undeterred. Now, he has developed two distinct products for the organic market: a perry, and an apple cider. In this orchard, at least, pears are the more straightforward candidates. 'We can use just a single variety of pear to make a perry. Even one veteran tree can provide a range of different traits; blending acidity, sweetness and drier, tannic qualities.' Apples can be a different matter. 'Most cider apples need blending, so we will often harvest from different kinds of tree.'

Just as the orchard birds benefit from its diversity of fruits and berries, so David's quest to keep the orchard traditional means that he benefits from the range of different local breeds that Nancy's family has nurtured and varied here for over four generations. Some, like the Broxwood Foxwhelp, one of the oldest varieties of cider-apple when found in its original cultivar, are strongly biennial; putting forward their bounty every other season. In such a diverse orchard, a number of different trees will conspire to give David the variety of apples that he needs. A Frederick will yield fruity, high-quality cider – but may not be stored for too long. The Dymock Red will inject a bittersharp taste to your brew, whereas a Sweet Alford, originally of Devon stock, provides the sugary biomass bulk needed to kick-start the fermentation process. The orchard's treasured Kingston Blacks, however, are not just veteran pieces of orchard history. From just this one breed, David often finds all the variety of apple tastes and textures needed to create a finely-balanced cider. The process of adjustment, learning and refinement continues every season but these ancient English breeds, even now, lie at the heart of the cider-making process.

Fruit farmers and cider-makers such as David, like the spotted flycatchers or honeybees in his orchard, were once common. Now he too is a critically-endangered species, hanging on against the odds. Around his farm, orchards continue to be grubbed out – as landowners and farmers cannot find a way to make them worthwhile. The apple mountain around me, though, seems to cry out the solution. Unlike our vanished hay meadows, traditional, homegrown orchards need not become one more museum piece in the dying British countryside. Instead, they could revitalise a whole sector of the farming community, taking nature with them as they go.

When it comes to food production, Britain leads the world in waste: waste on an epic and needless scale. According to the Produce Marketing Association, each year Britain imports 476,000 tonnes of apples from overseas; exporting just 14,800 tonnes, or 3 per cent of our domestic product, in return. As a country, our self-sufficiency in fruit is just 11 per cent, in a country once famed for its orchards – and still famous for its apples. Only 20 per cent of the apples we eat in Britain are grown in our own country.[1] It seems quite staggering, as I walk into a landscape carpeted in red and green fruit, of every different flavour, shape and taste, that Britain should ever import apples at all. We were once world leaders in the craft and production of native fruits – and, to the benefit of thousands of rural jobs, could be once again.

Yet while local orchards scream out a viable solution to revitalising rural economies and growing our own (two incentives we so often hear governments talk about), the odds are rigged against our traditional orchard growers at every turn. For decades, the European Union's Common Agricultural Policy has decimated orchards. It has paid for their removal and erased our natural heritage of traditional fruit-growing areas. The vanishing of our orchards, in truth, cannot be laid at the feet of individual farmers. Many orchard owners, like David, remain passionately attached to their fruit trees. But the EU has paid for orchards to be grubbed: dependent on its subsidies, farmers have, however reluctantly, followed suit. The great mass extinction policy for wildlife in our lifetimes has also, ironically, destroyed a generation of savvy, dedicated fruit growers – and their willingness to perpetuate the orchard song for future generations to enjoy.

The madness of ignoring our own, native fruits, and importing those from overseas, has been fuelled largely by the unnatural selection of our supermarkets – and the ignorance of governments in giving them free rein. Like something from an Orwellian vision or a Roald Dahl parody, many supermarkets have no interest in the rich heritage, taste and brilliance of the English apple. Instead, they demand wholly green apples, or those with a certain percentage of red. Apples are measured to within millimetres. Clones of conformity are the order of the day. The ramshackle beauty of English apple variety is lost on the mindless regulators who decide the fate of orchards in our country. If an English apple can keep forever, and doesn't readily bruise, then it can, on occasion, slip onto supermarket shelves. Flavour holds little sway in these cold calculations. England's apples grow slower, and therefore the taste develops and matures. Any orchard grower will explain that the gradual weathering of sun and rain gives our homegrown apples the best taste in the world. Yet in a country where new restaurants and food fashions take off every week, oddly few people seem to be aware of this, or care.

Instead of sponsoring the creation of fruit-growing areas across failing rural areas in our country, the combined unnatural selection of market and EU regulation now favours waxed imports that kill our climate, our wildlife and our rural jobs. On a global level, the damage wrought to our planet by our reliance on overseas apple suppliers, alone, is truly enormous. A single flight from New Zealand, one of our major apple suppliers, will pump over three tonnes of carbon into our planet's choking lungs. Meanwhile, our traditional orchards, their apples and pears sequestering carbon free of charge each day, perish every year.

As British people move more and more away from the consumption of red meat, and consume a third less milk than they did ten years ago, there is little sign that our appetite for fruit – or indeed cider – has remotely diminished. It is estimated, for example, that we consume 122 *thousand* tonnes of apples every year. The British demand for apples is insatiable – yet the viability of our orchards is not. Yet tantalisingly, this is the one form of farmland that we should sponsor most of all.

Whereas intensive dairy and sheep farming removes trees from the environment, denudes our grasslands of nectar and tramples and compacts our soils, passing chemicals from wormed animals deep into the ground, orchards sequester carbon, increase native fruit production, and guard soils that are teeming and intact. Unsprayed, as we have shown throughout this book that they can be, an orchard's wildlife might become simply the by-product of extraordinary agricultural productivity.

As Britain now leaves the European Union, how our country is farmed, and what farmland is paid for by us, may now be decided afresh. If we make the right decisions, then our orchards, their owners and their wildlife will be given the future they deserve.

It's early evening. Dazzling blue air and the musk-scent of rainy soil kicks me back into the wilder surroundings of the orchard. October is the month of preparation – and not just for its cider-making mammals. The freeze lies ahead. Nature scrambles to keep up – and the fallen apple bounty now receives more attention than ever.

Each afternoon, the windfalls of October concentrate a whole ecosystem of predators and prey within the crunchy carpet of the orchard's sheltered floor. By late evening, badgers slowly shuffle forth into the orchard – drawn to the bounty, in particular, of the Flakey Bark pear. Here, with the discernment of fine diners, the badgers remain so fond of this particular fruit that a latrine nearby shows the regularity of their visits. The influx of bank voles, field voles, wood mice and yellow-necked mice, chiselling away at the fallen fruits, draws in a host of predators. Buzzards can be seen perched unusually low in the wide-branched Strawberry Normans; waiting for an incautious or inebriated rodent to nail. Late evening sees teenage tawny owls, already being shifted out of their parents' territories, waiting patiently in the lower branches of the oaks in the certain knowledge that soon, the windfalls will be furry with food. October is a wonderful time for young owls.

In recent years, red admirals, which once migrated south into mainland Europe, are increasingly surviving our ever-milder winters, and in the orchard, the sugars they will need to see them through the hard times now lie in abundance on the ground. Here in Oak Orchard, where the apple fall lies thickest, the admirals' sweet tooth will often get the better of them. Like other larger *Nymphalids*, admirals are highly territorial. They circle piles of the rottenest apples with stiff, showy glides, before settling to drink. Competitors, even small ones, are not welcome. Bluebottle flies, attempting to land, are quickly dispelled with a disparaging flex of the wings; the cooler air current disturbing the fly's attempt to share the feast. Admirals are showy creatures – and they do not do things by halves. They will often drink well over the limit, and in contrast to their elegant reputation in the animal kingdom, these butterflies become drunk – and very disorderly.

Fermenting sugars in the fallen apples are converted

into ethanol as it is metabolised by the butterflies. As a result, the admirals become progressively more inebriated – and floppy. On occasion, the admirals must be picked up – and walked home. One butterfly took quite some time to recover when placed gently on a bough. On take-off, its flight was even more erratic than normal. In spite of these excesses, red admirals are born survivors – but making it through the winter will be their hardest challenge of all.

Only five of Britain's butterfly species will hibernate, as adults, through the winter: the red admiral, peacock, small tortoiseshell, brimstone and comma. On the face of it, the idea of these wafer-thin parcels of legs, veins and scales surviving snowfall seems little short of miraculous. The comma, in particular, has intrigued me for years. Anyone who can spot a comma with its wings closed, having no prior idea of its presence, is a better naturalist than I. Each autumn, the hedgerows of Hop Kiln Orchard abound with commas. One of our most familiar species, commas have not seen the same declines as many other garden favourites. In spite of their relative abundance, the comma's hibernation strategy remains almost entirely unknown. It is clear that when closed, commas mimic dead leaves – to an uncanny degree. The subtly changing shades of brown on the under-wing serve to perfectly break up their outline. Tauntingly, as far as the naturalist is concerned, commas are therefore believed to specialise in hibernating among dead leaves. A few have been found in honeysuckle tangles; others in coppiced hazel. I have spent many an hour patiently following comma butterflies along the orchard's hedgerows to resolve this mystery – and in every case, been profoundly defeated.

I have only found the red admiral's place of hibernation when, upon inspecting a new growth of mistletoe, I was startled to see what appeared to be a petrified pair of antennae protruding from the bark. It took a good minute for my mind to realise that I was looking at a roosting red admiral, its extraordinary lichen wings virtually invisible against the trunk. The admiral had wedged itself into a tiny nook of the tree, but it looked eerily fragile – sheltered from the elements, but exposed to the air. A silent statue, its stillness captivated me, yet I feared that it would perish come the first impending frosts.

Other butterfly species, we have found, seem to make more sensible decisions when choosing their winter home. As October cools, the applewood piles, many well crusted in bramble, nettle and ivy, become the focus of butterflies who, like the rest of the orchard's inhabitants, now make frenzied preparations for hibernation. But there are safer nooks yet.

Each October, if you were to look up from the cider press into the dark oak ceilings and beams of the hop kiln, you would see clusters of blackish leaves hanging upside-down. Over fifty peacock butterflies safely spend winter within this wooden cavern and its thermally-regulated refuge. In spite of sharing the ceiling with a colony of brown long-eared bats, the static, hanging butterflies are safe: bats use movement to hear their prey.

To even get to the stage of hibernation, butterflies like

peacocks have had to escape months of attention not only from spotted flycatchers, but from the orchard's enormous army of other insectivores, such as blue tits. It is thought peacocks do this by a combination of 'flashing' their false eyes on their forewings, with the production of a *hissing* noise. In one such study, only one of thirty-four peacock butterflies approached by a blue tit was eaten when this visual and sonic display was produced in tandem. The cruel scientists in the study, however, then painted over the peacock's 'eyes'. Most of the butterflies were immediately scoffed.

Judging the thermal insulation of one's home, and its chances of predation once sound asleep inside, soon becomes a matter of do or die for the orchard's peacocks. For those that do not discover the safety of the hop kiln, close watching suggests that each peacock butterfly exercises selective preference for the orchard's insulated nooks – and on a few special occasions, you get to watch a butterfly make up its mind. As the saying 'a butterfly mind' rightfully infers, it takes peacocks quite a while to reach a firm decision about their winter home.

I tuck myself onto a fallen bough, first casualty of the autumn winds – and watch. The peacock sallies around, turning suddenly as if some hidden kite-master pulls the strings. Tracking a butterfly is hard on the naked eye. I've chased butterflies since I was six, but their erratic movements, their best predator defense, exert the same visual confusion on the well-intentioned watcher. Now, the peacock reappears out of thin air, it would seem, some metres off the ground. With the sweeping glides that characterise the

Nymphalids, it inspects a series of cavities in a pear. One appears too shallow – it stalls only momentarily. It alights on another for some time, flexing its wings – and begins to crawl inside. What does it see? The angry glare of a hornet? The liquid, pale-eyed scrutiny of a jackdaw? Poor insulation? A second later, the peacock is back on the wing. For an hour it flaunts around, flirting with options – and then, with a purposeful dart, it glides onto the edge of a moss-aged green woodpecker nest hole. With little delay, it closes its wing – a lifeless-looking leaf – and stalks inside. Home – at last.

Quite how the orchard's butterflies physically survive the winter is one of those engaging little stories that plays out largely unseen, as we walk past and fail to notice the orchard's wintering statues. This peacock, like all of Britain's hibernating butterflies, will rely on antifreeze to get it through the winter. Blood sugar, now of little use as the insect will not be expending energy, is converted instead into glycerol. Dormant in the dark, this chemical compound will help regulate the body temperature of the butterfly. This is the last line of hibernatory defence; buying the peacock a degree or two of vital extra warmth. The tree caves of the orchard, particularly the chasms dug by green woodpeckers, which can penetrate the old pears by more than half a metre, provide the perfect thermal residence for its wintering peacocks. And our admiration for the role played by the orchard's aerial beavers only increases as the butterflies go to bed.

The hedgerows heave with the embers of haws and the crimson of rosehips, while wild crab apples fall softly within their thorny walls. The pinks, black and whites of the Hop Kiln Orchard's long-tailed tit family – two adults and still seven surviving young – bounce through the hawthorns as they feed up for the lean times; the tail, it always seems, wagging the bird.

With Nancy's permission, we carefully collect the hips to make rosehip jelly; scolded by the sad, mournful whistles of a pair of bullfinches. Reproached, we call off our foraging and retreat, allowing the hedgerow's conveyor belt of birds to move in. Hips are visited, though not as much as haws. Long ago, the peoples of Anglo-Saxon England recognised the importance of these *hagu-berige*,[2] or hedge-berries. Packed with Vitamin C, haws provide a rare bounty at the onset of winter. Now is the time of year when the orchard's bullfinches begin to shine. The dual flashes of white rumps denote the tightly-bonded pairs as they fly everywhere, feeding everywhere, together. Of all the orchard's birds, none form more intricate pair-bonds than the bullfinch. It has been observed that male bullfinches, in captivity, if they lose their partners, may become so unaccustomed to singing that they entirely forget how to do so.

The only red that burns more deeply than the orchard's rose hips is the scarlet breast of the male bullfinch, as, throwing habitual summer caution to the winds, he gorges openly on haws. Lean, sour and dry to our taste, these berries form an invaluable transitory food source that helps bullfinches, one of our hardiest resident birds, make it through the winter, without leaving the tiny territories where they are born, raised and die.

Bullfinches are not only dazzling birds to look at, when finally seen well, but come equipped with a very special arsenal for giving fruiting trees or bushes a hard time. Their secateur bills can make short work of up to thirty flower buds per minute, and as such, they were condemned for their 'criminal attacks' on fruit trees by Henry VIII. During medieval times, food security was demanded by royal decree. In a time of frequent wars, it was the responsibility of all to ensure that any wild beast threatening food production was destroyed, with bounties paid out by parish churches for dead specimens. Species that specialised in feeding on any part of an orchard tree were killed in their droves. Charm and attractiveness did nothing to reduce the tenacity of these attacks, as witnessed by the plight of the humble bullfinch.

Roger Lovegrove documents the barely believable scale of this assault in his book, *Silent Fields*. Despite their diminutive presence – often only signalled by a subtle *'pew-pewww'* fluting from deep within a blackthorn and bramble thicket – bullfinches are specialists at de-budding fruit trees; their stubby beak particularly suited to removing the protein-rich bud from young fruit on pear and plum trees. This was enough to earn them a place on the list of 'noysome fowles' that should be destroyed, with the same bounty placed on their heads as for ravens and red kites. Lovegrove's detailed research of old parish bounty payment records uncovered just how many bullfinches were eradicated as part of this targeted campaign. The record was at Rostherne in Cheshire, where the barely believable total of 819 were killed in 1687 in just 900 acres. Unlike with larger bird species such as magpies, where ground traps were used, the favoured method used to trap bullfinches was limed twigs – sited in places where the birds regularly perched; effectively gluing down the birds as they landed, ensuring a prolonged and agonising death. The fact bullfinches were able to be caught like this gives away the sheer abundance of this now infrequently seen species. At the same time, the idea of a frequent and generic 'bullfinch perch' – in the way that a peregrine might be loyal to a particular plucking post – isn't known today, so it's likely a fair number of other species were taken as bycatch in efforts to reduce bullfinch numbers.[3]

Fortunately, despite still being under general licence to orchard growers until 1998 – before which bullfinches were allowed to be destroyed – the species has now been offered full protection from persecution. Yet the densities with which bullfinches were formerly present remind us that conditions for them now are very different to those of a few hundred years ago. Bullfinches thrive only when scrub is allowed to develop, growing well above the level of Britain's generally stunted, lashed hedgerows and into thorn castles towering several metres in height. As a result, the orchard's blackthorn hedges hold half a dozen pairs of these secretive songsters, fluting their sombre tunes from enormous hedgerows. Today, it is not the destruction of the bullfinches themselves, but of the cavernous hedgerows they frequent that threatens their survival.

For me and Nick, as for many other naturalists across the country, the annual October destruction of hedgerows – as nature is given its worst ever haircut – is one of the most senseless acts of vandalism that we, as a nation, have become accustomed to in recent decades. Such destruction continues at large across our country. In the slashed, stunted metre-high hedgerows that increasingly constitute the norm, bullfinches, warblers, marsh tits and many other ancient hedgerow denizens need not apply. If this continues, ever fewer children will get to see glowing autumn hedgerows in their unbridled finery.

The chilling, mathematical hedge-lines we see in most of Britain today are entirely useless to most of our scrub-evolved wildlife. A bullfinch hedgerow, or one sympathetic to warblers such as lesser whitethroats, becomes joyously overgrown and dense not over one but closer to fifteen years. And for marsh tits to place their nests near the roots of a cavernous hazel, and dormice to creep through its dense branches, a hedgerow must burgeon for more like thirty years; growing to well over five metres high – and deep.

For barbastelle bats to colonise the cavities of outgrown oaks, aspiring through generations to break the shackles of hedgerow life, that hedgerow must be well over a century old. The billowing, drooping stands of cuckoo-haunted willow that still grace the Malvern countryside, as they once did all of the British landscape, lining the rivers at the orchard's edge, are well over two hundred years in age. It's been a long time since these imposing willows called themselves a hedge. But with our hedgerows shorn each winter, the next generation of giants are never being given the chance to begin their journey.

The enormous dependence of birds on an ever-changing bounty of light-loving, berry-bearing scrub trees, is a reminder that Britain's fauna developed in a world of space and light, where herbivore-hammered thorn-lands would have been an intregral part of the ecosystem. Indeed, while the orchard is man-made, the alliances and relationships we watch in our autumn hedgerows are ancient and profound, far predating our ecologically recent colonisation of these islands.

Rarely now, however, do you see crab apple and elder, blackthorn and wild rose, hawthorn and cherries, all tangled together in a towering fortress, jostling with fruits, each selling their wares to an insatiable market of native buyers. Trashed by many of our local councils and some, though by no means all, of our farmers, the flailed hedgerows of modern Britain form the ecological equivalent of pruning back the rainforest to one metre high.

Each autumn, this lawful destruction of hedgerows around us robs millions of birds, rodents and insects of potential homes and food, just as nature's richest wares have been put on display. But here, in the orchard, we are buffered from the senseless compulsion to tidy the land and starve our wilder neighbours. October is a month of hyper-abundance, where every scruffy orchard inch yields life.

Having been left for two years at a time, to provide a dense haven for foxes, hedgehogs, beetles, dunnocks and dozens of other orchard denizens, a few selected log piles will now be burned – ahead of the hibernation season. Nancy and David meticulously remove the branches, one at a time. If anything stirs within, they retreat. One large pile remains intact. This is home to 'the rabbit': a well-known and bouncy hedgehog of legendary stature. Fattened on slugs and apples, he has made Oak Orchard's largest pile of brash his winter home.

Elsewhere, unwieldy clumps of moss-encrusted apple boughs are now brought to the burner. Here, even the lost limbs and ghost branches of the orchard will be put to good use; sold as a sustainable source of charcoal. Loaded into the black kiln, the fire is lit. The warming, cinnamon kick of apple smoke soaks the air as the wind rises.

Almost out of time, a twitter of swallows cling to the swaying wires next to the hop kiln. It's late. Most swallows depart Britain in September, but the bite of autumn has been delayed. The parents look worn and exhausted. Flexing their wings eagerly, their second batch of children simply look hungry. The family have been hoovering the rich skies all week long; quietly helping David as they snatch agricultural pests from the orchard's airways. As many as seven hundred insects can be taken by one swallow in the course of a single day.

In Victorian times, records of swallows in late autumn and winter were so rare that some early naturalists thought they hibernated at the bottom of ponds. Now, in our warming climate, a small but growing number of swallows will winter on our coasts. Higher temperatures than in years gone by mean that some may find more insect food, even in the harshest of months. Yet these warmer winter temperatures, that allow swallows to stay on our shores, will also fail to kill the dozens of diseases that could decimate the trees in our adopted orchard. In temperate Europe, winter is *supposed* to be cold. Britain's unseasonal swallows are a disturbing sign. I hope dearly these will not become winter swallows – for them, and for us.

As the wind rises, the glowing autumn air finally seems to cool. And the swallows really must be gone. They will soon travel not only south of the Equator but as far south as Kwazalu-Natal, in South Africa. From the Malverns, these twittering leaves, taken now by the gust of wind that punches them skywards off the hop kiln wires, have 9,500 kilometres of flying left ahead. With any luck, this brood will return here the following year; another 20,000 kilometres of air miles on the clock. They spiral up, up, as the oak leaves fall. Higher, higher, until they are lost in the piercing blue.

Deep sun meets leaves and apple smoke – and all things merge. The orchard air glows amber. The static hiss of golden fallen leaves rushes through the smoke as the fieldfares blow in, cackling with glee at the windfalls of winter.

NOVEMBER

THE END OF THE FEAST

BEN

The bees argue, in their black ball,
A flying hedgehog, all prickles.

SYLVIA PLATH

It has not only been a good year for the apple crop. Both the oak and beech around the orchard have yielded exceptional riches. While all trees that produce fruits or seeds have good years, bad years and many, like some pear and apple breeds, fruit in alternate years, few fluctuate so dramatically as beech or oak. The mystery of the mast has intrigued biologists for years. Often, in the same year, these giants of the British woodland will put out huge volumes of seeds, carpeting the woodland floor with a sudden bounty of food. The next few years will often be quiet ones, with little fruition whatsoever.

211

Given that putting out acorns increases an oak's chances of reproduction, why not do this every year? This comes down in part to sheer effort. For a giant that lives for several hundred years, putting out a huge volume of acorns every year is energy-intensive. Better to save resources for every five, even ten years, and then give the gardeners the ammunition needed to further the future of your own kind. Secondly, by putting out so many seeds at once, these trees ensure their edible wares flood the market – ensuring not all can be taken by an insatiable army of autumn foragers.

In these mast years, the ground below the oaks crawls with foragers. Nuthatches and great spotted woodpeckers, glowing in the shade, move unobtrusively through the mast, selecting choice acorns. Occasionally, they will burst upwards, like reverse leaf-fall, as a sparrowhawk steers through the apples' maze on its swift and deadly course; long tail navigating it through the smallest of openings between the trees.

As November dawns, you have to watch your head. Falling apples are the least of your concerns. Huge snags can, and do, fall from the oldest fruit trees. These, in turn, are mere twigs compared to the twisted, scarred limbs of oaks that fall from time to time. But another sound you become conscious of, if sitting for some time in one place, is the soft but certain 'pshhtt' of falling acorns. Many of these tumble from the magnificent aged giants in Oak Orchard. Other acorns, however, fall from a clear blue sky! The orchard's master forester is hard at work.

Silent and furtive throughout the late summer months,

our local 'wood-screechers' (the Welsh name being *Ysgrech y Coed*) ramp up the volume. Of all the birds in the orchard, it is only in recent years that we have come to cherish and appreciate the importance of the jay. Where bird populations are already tiny and fractured, nest-raiding jays can become problematic for those species – but in the healthy, food-rich ecosystem of the orchard, we have never found jays to affect any of the orchard's smaller birds, such as spotted flycatchers, in the long term. Nests are raided, chicks are eaten, but the jays here are kept in check as well, and must avoid at all costs the blood-red stare of the goshawk. Far from a menace, the jay is a cornerstone species; a vital life force in the world of the orchard.

Garrulus glandarius, the 'chattering acorn gatherer', is a lifelong friend of the orchard's oaks. At this time of year, you can sit and soak in their salmon hues and azure flashing wings as they strip their way through the crown of the Ancient Ones in Oak Orchard. It is only when you set up a camouflage hide, a telescope, and lavishly scatter acorns on a fallen branch, however, that you get to watch these wary hoarders at work. Head cocked as it lands, the jay looks sceptical. It's as if someone has put down a large hoard of acorns in one place. Soon, however, its base instincts get the better of its fiendishly smart brain. The jay swallows one acorn, then another, then another. It's a little like watching rabbits disappear into a rather small hat. Like their North American cousins, Eurasian jays have evolved elastic, expandable throats – specifically for this reason. This allows them to safely store multiple acorns in their crop ahead of making a single trip to stash their bounty away. The evolution makes perfect sense; having to take each of one's shopping items away separately would be time-intensive and waste critical energy. Watchful of the small army of grey squirrels around it, my jay swallows four acorns. The fifth is the one that it keeps carried in its bill. This jay, it turns out, is a little above average. Jays will usually carry three acorns per trip – but the most impressive of their kind can carry up to nine. In a salmon-coloured flash, it bounds off across the golden apple carpet.

Animals that hoard are split into two general categories – 'scatter hoarders' and 'larder hoarders'. We as humans are larder hoarders. Unless possessed of unusual social traits, we rarely scatter food at dozens of locations around our houses and gardens. Jays, however, take the opposite approach. While small larders have on occasion been studied, each individual jay – capable of storing five thousand acorns in the course of a winter – will generally cache these in a baffling range of different sites. With around ten jays, parents and young on the wing by October, this means that around fifty thousand acorns will be stashed in and around the orchard each autumn. Some will be wedged securely in cracks in the bark, others buried in the ground (jays may have to dig through a foot of snow to get these out). It has previously been held that jays, being mere birds, forget about a lot of the acorns that they stash, while dropping others by accident. These, of course, are the acorns that can grow, over time, into oaks. But what if this, too, wasn't an accident? What if jays *didn't* forget?

Scientists curious about those 'forgotten' acorns have returned to watch what happens the following spring. Jays, they found, return to many newly planted oak saplings within their territories. They then actively defoliate the young oak leaves, carry them off, and feed them to their newly hatched chicks. These nutritious fledgling oak leaves, known as cotyledons, are unique – jays do not take the young leaves of other species, nor can their chicks digest the leaves of a mature oak. This fresh salad for their infants is harvested from the very trees grown from acorns cached the previous autumn and winter. In other words, rather than forgetting stashed acorns by accident, there is strong evidence to show that these avian geniuses leave them by design.[1]

We humans often credit other animals with great intelligence only with extreme reluctance. We now know that elephants can feel profound emotional connection to the graveyards of their kin, transmit messages seismically through the very earth itself, and detect distant lightning storms. We are just beginning to understand the depth of communication in killer whales, the memory of octopuses and the twenty-year learning curve of one of our closest relatives, an infant orangutan. Jays, hunted almost to extinction by Victorian gamekeepers, have escaped our admiration rather more. Yet this hugely intelligent forester has been shaping the very landscape where we live and walk, with an eerie degree of foresight, for hundreds of thousands of years.

The actions of jays in scattering oaks has been proven to be far more valuable than the actions of foresters in planting them – all in one cluster, at one time. A Polish study in the Bialowieza Forest showed that oaks growing singly, scattered by jays over a wide area, have a much greater chance of survival than oak saplings planted in one place.[2] It should indeed be obvious that no known living or historical animal has ever planted trees in neat rows. Oaks are designed to grow far and wide, reducing the species' chances of early defoliation by mammalian herbivores. Jays are the only foresters to make this happen.

Every time you pass an oak pushing through a verdant hedgerow, protected by its thorns – be thankful for the jay. Oak trees and jays enjoy a symbiosis developed over millions of years. Writ large, the action of jays in the Malverns' tree-rich landscape, where they are rarely hunted any more, shapes the leafy aspect of these softly wooded hills. The amount of new oak in the landscape, pushing through dense blackthorn, growing on hillsides free from overgrazing, or bursting through bramble in the sunlit glades around the orchard, is a continuous signal of hope for Nick and me. We readily forgive our jays the few nests raided in the orchard that summer as, come the next spring, new oaks rise magically around the orchard's walls.

Indeed, as we look around, it occurs to us that almost every ancient oak in the orchard would, in fact, have been planted by a jay. The oaks are ancient hedge-markers, and they too would have grown through the dense blackthorns now long vanished from their shade. Because oaks grow best when protected by thorns, sky-dropped acorns, not human planting, would have allowed the acorn to drop into a tangle of thorns and, unreachable by cattle, grow through the hedgerow of that time – and out into the light.

Flapping overhead on rounded wings, jays are Europe's

premiere avian foresters. They should, in our view, be protected by the very best legislation that there is – because they are nature's most effective means of reforesting our island.

As the oaks teem with the merchants of the mast, so the hedgerows grow thick with sloes and song thrushes. From elders in August to the scarlet protein parcels of rosehips and haws in September and October, the dominant colour come early November is the alluring deep purples of the sloe. Moving along these purple lines, dozens of redwings 'zip' call as they bound away down the hedge-line. The belligerent fieldfares are back, defending whole bushes against their smaller competitors. Song thrushes, mistle thrushes, starlings and blackbirds can all be watched, over the course of an hour, piling in to snatch the vivid, midnight-coloured fruits.

While we who harvest the British hedgerow may be able to make sloe gin from these verdant winter berries, jellies from rosehips and wine from elderflowers, it is odd how, as the descendants of hunter-gatherers, we appear poorly adapted to enjoy much of the 'raw' berry product, if compared to the rampant birds that would once have competed with us for this winter protein resource. Rosehips contain powder that makes our skin physically uncomfortable to such a degree that it was the original ingredient of itching powder. Tucking into a haw is no pleasant experience. Consuming an elder berry, for most people, packs a bitter and astringent punch to the palate. Fellow mammalian omnivores of the Eurasian temperate woodlands, such as brown bears, have developed no such culinary qualms. It seems we have grown accustomed, perhaps for a long time indeed, to manicuring these winter fruits and turning them into products of greater satisfaction to our taste buds. As I sit watching and musing on the vagaries of human taste, it occurs to me to pick some sloes from the hedgerow. On closer inspection, it is just as well I am not collecting for a cave-load of my peers. The thrushes have scoffed the lot.

It's mid afternoon. The crystal-clear fluting of robins marks out the next shift in the orchard's ever changing seasons. It's a sound forgotten since spring, but all the stranger for hearing now only male and female sopranos of one species singing in unison, when all the other choristers have fallen silent. Robins are unique in many ways, but there is nothing more distinctive than their winter song.

Robins are lifelong residents of the orchard. Come August heatwave or February snowstorm, they haunt the ivy-covered walls of the hop kiln, the dense brambles of the hedge-lines, and the woodpecker caverns they sometimes adopt as their summer homes. As a result, both males and females remain territorial through the winter months. And both sing vociferously, passionately, in defence of their winter homes.

Robins being so well known, scientists have spent many years investigating the science behind the piercing winter song that is often the orchard's only soundtrack at this time of year. By simulating incursion into robin territory, it has been found that both males and females aggressively defend their patch – but in different ways. In summer, the male alone will defend the breeding territory, showing heightened levels of testosterone. At this time, females have low levels of testosterone but high levels of ovarian oestrogen, as you would expect for a mother preparing to lay up to six eggs. In winter, this all changes. Females get really pumped up. Their aggression levels soar – and therefore the most vocal robin now singing in the hop-kiln garden, I came to realise, was just as likely to be *her.*

Behind the autumnal fluting lies a chemically-infused world of aggression. During winter, females and males, whatever their past marital relations, do not team up to share territories. Each defends his or her own. Bachelor males, perhaps unsurprisingly, sing less than mated males whose females produce at least one family in the course of a season. Even though males sing in winter, it is now the females who are charged up with plasma testosterone. In fact, come October, a male robin's winter testosterone levels are low. Indeed, testosterone influences the nature of his song throughout the year. In the breeding season, his complex notes are infused with sexual invitation; a love song ravaged by hormones. Come autumn and winter, his song, now simplified, is more of an angry soprano refrain: 'keep out'. In spite of this, male and female robins, as you would expect, can differentiate at all times between who is singing. Males in autumn have been found to react angrily, and quickly, to the song of another male; coming in to chase off the intruder. Males will also attack stuffed robins, used to gauge their reactions, with considerably more violence than most of us might attack a burglar in our homes. These winter robins, mellifluous as they may sound, are no less aggressive than a Doberman guard dog; poised, fluid, ready – to warn, bark and ultimately strike.[3]

Each evening from hereon, as the autumn ambers grow, the orchard robins begin to sing more and more after dark. In the urban world, it is not light pollution, so much as daytime noise, that renders robins increasingly reliant on singing at night. Drowned out in their cities by day, acoustic interference frustrates these most vocal of choristers. Only as human traffic dies down can urban robins make themselves heard. In the orchard, however, there is little daytime noise from humans. Even David's harvesting is a quiet activity. But there *is* a veritable wall of *avian* sound. The babble of apple-drunk starling gangs and chortling fieldfares pushes a sonar wave outward from the orchard. It is hard to be certain, but watching the hop-kiln robins turn up the volume as the sun goes down, I wonder if they are finally able to hear themselves sing – as the cackling winter hoarders tuck themselves up for the night.

Come mid-November, the haws have now fallen – and a new hedgerow saviour comes to the fore. The ivy is in blossom. Maligned and cut down in so many of our gardens, ivy flourishes in ancient hedge-lines – and the thick, dead oaks in the Maze Orchard hedgerow provide the perfect trellis for the orchard's ivy to grow rampant. Ivy deceives the human eye for most of the year. It lies dormant, deep and waxy green; unglamorous and often little liked. Two of the greatest modern myths about ivy are that it damages walls – and kills trees. On closer inspection, it has been found that ivy creates a thermal blanket; its shiny leaves insulating its internal reaches against the cold. This, of course, is one of the reasons that ivy forms such an invaluable refuge for hibernating insects. For the same reason, it can protect a wall from the ravages of the winter frost; and the same goes for oak trees, too. Only when a dead oak's burden becomes unbearable, and the tree is already old and weak, can ivy and a strong wind conspire to bring it down.

By early November, the ivy, on close inspection, has become fussy with fast-moving action. Hoverflies are thick on the ivy blossom. The autumn's last butterflies – weary speckled woods and a few late-flying holly blues – feed with all the desperation of this being the final banquet of the year. By the middle of the month, however, ivy puts its best, fast-creeping foot forwards. Only when all other trees and flowers fail the orchard's denizens does it clamber to the fore: the latest-opening restaurant in town. The presence of ivy single-handedly determines the survival of many British species across a winter's course.

One of Herefordshire's newest colonists has been quick to arrive here. Ivy bees were only first reported in Britain in 2001, but have rapidly spread northwards into the Welsh Marches. With ample time, you can pick out their slender golden forms hovering in the shade. Females each have their own burrow, but unlike many solitary bees, they do nest close together. One September, in the disturbed soils at the base of the big ivy oak, I found a colony – and discovered the closest thing nature has to a rugby scrum. Males know that the females must emerge from their burrows – and unceremoniously doorstep them as they pop out. What follows, very quickly, is a buzzing, squirming golden ball. Many males pile onto a single female, and then one another, in a frenzied and often frustrated attempt to mate. The ball rolls around on the ground in strange, comical yet deadly serious combat. For hours, there can be chaos as the males all seek to chuck one another off the mating pile and get to the hapless and increasingly squashed female underneath. And then, moments later, the scrum will disperse. For those who do not spend large periods of time with their head inside a hedge, such a phenomenon can pass us by each autumn – not only in ancient orchards but even the ivy that still grows beside our villages and gardens.

Yet the ivy bee's northwards push is perhaps for the same reason that our swallows are so late leaving, our red admirals no longer departing southwards, tired butterflies are still on the wing, and why, right now, the 'chiff-chiff-chaff' beside me, crisp as the autumn air, can still be heard. Like our blackcaps, chiffchaffs are now spending the winter in the orchard, and each year their numbers appear to increase, as ever fewer make the journey south to winter in Spain. The world warms. The orchard, and its seasons, are changing – and fast.

As November hardens and thickens with the first frosts, the process of ageing in the orchard's veteran apples accelerates. As these trees senesce, one of the most important organisms in the orchard's life cycle will bloom come early winter. Fungi play an invaluable role in the biodiversity of the orchard. And one of the great secrets to their perseverance lies in the very nature of an orchard's soil.

Fungal circuit-boards buried below our feet conspire to form a *mycorrhiza:* a symbiotic relationship between the rhizome root systems of particular plants, and the fungus itself. Unlike the orchard's hapless hoverflies, the relationship between fungus and plants is one based around shared benefits. By growing on and within the root systems of a plant, mycorrhizal fungi benefit by receiving a regular feed of carbohydrates, such as glucose and sucrose, from the plant's roots. In turn, plants can struggle, unaided, to gain crucial access to soil micronutrients, such as iron. The fungi however, aid the plants in this regard. Their mycelium – the vegetative, thread-like hyphal webs – can access ions in the soil and render trace materials, such as iron, readily available to the plant. Plants in this orchard, therefore, are reliant not on chemical phosphates pumped into the soil each season, but rather, on social networking with the orchard's fungal internet.

This unseen relationship, however, goes much further. Plants with mycorrhizal associations are often more resistant to disease. Nematode worms, which can decimate root systems, can be repelled by toxins excreted into the soil by the mycorrhizae embedded in or around the roots of a plant. The excretion of such toxins then activates the plant's immune system, enabling it to better repel attack.

What has come to light even more recently is that plants may use fungal networks to produce and receive warning signals between themselves; effectively creating a bush-telegraph system within the soil itself. If attacked by an aphid, a mycorrhizal plant will signal an 'SOS' to those in the vicinity; morse code reverberating down the fungal network to its peers. In response, the plants receiving this distress call will release VOCs – volatile organic compounds. These work to attract the predators of the tiny nibbling attackers. If attacked, for example, by the orchard's plentiful *Spodoptera* (small 'pest' moths that also eat away at apple leaves), plants will release strongly-odoured chemical emissions known as terpenes. These will often rapidly recruit predatory wasps, first drawn to the scent and then to the hapless moths in question. If one plant wired into the orchard's fungal broadband comes under attack, others will immediately begin their chemical release.

The orchard's veteran apple trees, too, talk quietly among themselves below the soil – sharing secrets and plans whose results we will only see years later. The apples either produce a windfall one year – or yield barely any fruit at all. Everything from environmental stress, or predation attempts upon their leaves, to the urge to put forth fruit is shared via the hyphal network deep below our feet. Remarkable as this is, we still remain ignorant about the subtleties of tree conversation, and perhaps there is something rather special in how well they keep their conversations hidden from us; far better, indeed, than most of us keep our social secrets hidden from one another.

Such intensely complex relationships between plants, trees and fungi, unseen below the soil, are increasingly endangered in the fractured soilscapes of the British countryside. Deep ploughing, in many of our farmed environments, leads to the long-term disruption of life within the soil – particularly the networks of fungal hyphae below the ground that allows plants and trees to converse.

Traditional orchards, however, are very distinctive in the world of produce-growing. Many have never been ploughed at all. Indeed, it is impossible to plough an orchard without risking severe damage to the very roots of the trees that you protect. Our adopted orchard, like other ancient orchards here in Herefordshire and Worcestershire, acts as one of the last protectors of a subterranean world; a fungal morse-code system of enormous complexity, which protects the very plants within it, and the nectar-based food-chain on which the orchard's pollinators depend.

Come November, from a busy world below the soil, varied fruiting bodies spring: the visible canopy of the orchard's fungal rainforest. The shaggy scalycap froths from the base of the oldest apple trunks; its fruits coated like the aniseed frost on a white-iced bun, or the soft-feathered mantle of a barn owl. An odour of crisp radish wafts from it: tempting, perhaps, were it not known to have caused several cases of poisoning. The scalycap grows profusely wherever an old tree has ripped itself from the ground during November's frequent gales, or been reluctantly felled by Nancy and David. Often, soon after a tree has fallen, its glutinous clusters can be seen adorning the giant's point of execution. Edible chicken-of-the-woods fungus, a wildwood species associated with open-grown trees, can be found sprouting, like withered slices of orange, from the sides of old cherries and pears. It purportedly tastes like chicken: we've yet to put this to the test. Veterans like the old Kingston Black now bristle with a fungus known as shaggy bracket. A flattened syrup steam pudding of a mushroom, its sugary orange growth conceals a subterranean city below as its hyphae probe deep, hollowing the tree's decaying heart.

As the year mellows and dies, the breakdown of the orchard's fallen giants will begin. The visible and subterranean fungal network now gets to work decomposing the decaying trees and branches. The hyphal tentacles secrete acids and extracellular enzymes which act to break down nutrients: nutrients that the fungi will then reabsorb. Cellulase, an enzyme secreted from fungal tentacles, sinks deep into the orchard's dead timbers – and accelerates their decay. The hyphae are powerful burrowers, delving deep into the wood at speeds of forty micrometres per minute. By doing so, secreting as they go, fungal hyphae not only make short work of the orchard's soft apple wood, relentlessly pushing it apart, but are so small, numerous and strong that they can even break apart and break down solid rock.

After a veteran apple has fallen, valuable, tough cellular resources remain locked, inert, within its boughs. Cellulose, a long-chain molecule, is the most abundant on our planet – and what gives living trees their fortress-like strength. Lignin, a polymer that provides strength to cell walls, and longevity to plant cells, is also extremely tough to break down. This is where the orchard's hyphae also get to work. As they chemically gnaw away at the fallen apple's very molecular chains, the fungi impart small, nutrient-rich molecules back into the soil. Broken down, the next generation of plants, and trees, can now access these in order to grow. Nitrogen and phosphorus are not naturally abundant on our planet. So fungi wrestle these scant resources from the fallen – and return them, through the soil, to the next generation of the living.

So great is the importance of fungi to the orchard's soils that it even makes its way into the heart of the cider-making process. David does not use sulphites in his cider. Sulphites are designed to deal with microbiological contamination; the result of rot within the apples. But with little rot in the pest-cleansed orchard, David relies, instead, on wild yeasts.

Two theories have been put forward for how wild yeasts, which are not deliberately introduced by traditional cider-makers, find their way into the fermentation process. The first is that yeasts colonise fallen fruit from the ground. The second, that the very action of milling and pressing the fruit moves natural microscopic yeasts from the wooden beams and into the cider itself. Whatever the explanation, deep within the hop kilns' quiet ranks of amber jars, fungi, in the form of wild yeasts, will help ferment the cider throughout the winter; proving the invaluable agent of decomposition not only of the orchard's fallen trees – but of its most important export.

Microscopic cavities, forming fast within the decaying wood of the orchard, will soon become the homes for a rotting underworld of life; a fermenting forest, whose biodiversity is so rich that it is now regarded as being of national importance. In recent years, close examination of the Malverns' ancient orchards by specialists has uncovered a dizzying array of saproxylic, or wood-dwelling invertebrates.

As the orchards of the Malverns have matured, wood-decay specialists have been able to move in and thrive in the apples, pears and cherries. These trees have come to blend seamlessly with the decaying stands of oaks, willows and other ancients – creating a wood pasture landscape both original and planted. Confined, encrypted within these orchards, lie ecosystems far richer than most of us could imagine: depositories of species rescued from extinction; refugees of an older world.

Hiding within the deadwood of the Malverns' ancient orchards, entomologists are uncovering new denizens of decay. One hide beetle, *Megatoma undata*, specialises only in scavenging the spider webs found within the decaying wood of old trees. It feasts on the dried remnants of flies – long after the spider has sucked them dry. The false darkling beetle is so fussy that it develops only within the brackets of the shaggy bracket fungus, as this, in turn, takes root on apple heartwood. A fungus gnat, *Acnemia amoena*, not known from Herefordshire before recent surveys here, appears to feast only amid wood-decaying fungi. The larvae of the cobweb beetle develops only in the dank, spider's-web-filled cavities of thick, decaying bark. In its early stages, the large fruit tree bark beetle develops below the freshly dead bark of decaying fruit trees. One false click beetle, *Eucnemis capucina*, was so rare that it was largely known from the most ancient pasture woods of the New Forest; now, it has been found to haunt these orchards' cherry trees as they decay. Another beetle, *Aulonothroscus brevicollis*, was known only from twelve ancient parklands in southern England; now it, too, has joined the Malvern orchard list. So specialised are many of these deadwood denizens, they might seem more suited to the niches of a tropical rainforest than modern farmland Britain.[4]

As I wander around the orchard towards the end of November, and pause to inspect the bulging shaggy bracket fungus on the old Kingston Black, it feels as though I am standing in an untapped ecosystem as complex as that of the Amazon, where decay itself promotes the greatest life of all. Yet this orchard has stood for fewer than a hundred years. Most of its standing trees were planted after 1930.

The speed with which orchards age has brought salvation to creatures of the wild wood drawn to the richness of decay – whether beetles or fungi, bats or woodpeckers. Yet the same speed of decay is, right now, proving to accelerate the downfall of traditional orchards. As I look around, another four apple trees have come down in the gales. Two of these were standards in their prime; felled not by age but by waterlogged soils, as their roots have failed to anchor their vessel upright. An aggressive robin, female perhaps, sings from the unearthed cluster of its backlit sky-bound roots.

While decay has driven the diversity of our adopted orchard, cycled nutrients back into its soil and helped populate the fruit groves with life, orchards are fragile places for these very same reasons. These ecosystems are forests with a shelf-life of no more than sixty years; unable to sustain themselves without the care, investment and time of their human foresters.

Come the evening, we light the log fire and the glorious incense of burning apple wood ignites the room. Sitting down with Nancy, David and the Mogster, who now toasts himself smugly by the fireside, the orchard's trustees get to work mapping out the tree-planting to be done in the months ahead. At the end of the orchard year, December must bring a new generation of life – if the orchard we have come to love is to stand the trials of winters to come.

DECEMBER

THE NEXT GENERATION

BEN

Even if I knew that tomorrow
the world would go to pieces,
I would still plant my apple tree.

MARTIN LUTHER

Each winter, concealed under the cover of darkness, a team of earthmovers will arrive in a now derelict, overgrown orchard on the eastern edge of the Forest of Dean. Freezing and alert, we tuck into the side of a hedge and wait for the portable diggers to arrive. Time passes slowly when it's this cold. Soon, the dazzling silver of the moon grows so bright in the clear sub-zero sky that we can see quite clearly in the dark. Moon shadows stretch the sagging apple trees towards us. A tawny owl hoots, once, then reconsiders: even owls do not like it this cold. Badgers will be snoring deep within their setts. Our target animal, however, thrives as far north as Siberia. It does not hibernate. It is unstoppable.

Given the impressive size of the male, the appearance of the wild boar family in the moonlight is silent, quiet; almost apologetic. Their poor eyesight failing them, they take some time to adjust to the open aspect of the orchard; acute noses probe the air for even a whiff of trouble – but we are downwind. In Britain, boar currently have no predators – except us.

The boar act with extreme wariness as they slowly move into the orchard. Over a decade of human hunting here in the Forest of Dean has rendered many populations nocturnal refugees. Now they gain confidence – and the earth-moving begins. The enormous male, separate from what looks to be a more cautious family group behind him, begins tearing up the grass below the trees; rolling back huge sods of earth to expose the fertile soil below. In a single night, he will make light work of the orchard lawn; turning the ground below the now rotting windfalls into a battlefield. By dawn, deeper furrows will reveal where particularly tasty morsels have been rootled out. These boar are responding to the instructions of one of the most powerful noses in the animal kingdom. Drawn in by the far-drifting sweet liqueur of fermenting fruit, the well-loved winter combination of pork and apple now comes together in a wholly different way.

As we watch, though, the boar abandon their familiar rootling habits – and turn their attention to the accessible rotting apples instead. Their discernment in which apples they choose is of interest. While we have never witnessed this ourselves, those studying animal cognition in Switzerland have found that boar prefer to wash their food, particularly fruit, before consuming it.[1] When presented with clean apples, the boar in the study promptly ate them. When presented with dirty ones, they would often take food to water, or use their own saliva to remove excess grit and dirt, which could damage their teeth. Tonight, it seems the rain-washed apples are to their liking; they move around quietly, hoovering up the sugary bounty. The boar have struck lucky: in many of our modern forests, you rarely find so many fruit trees in one place.

Of Europe's remaining ecosystem architects, wild boar are one of our most important 'endozoochorous' dispersers. This means boar can excrete fruit seeds that have passed through their gut over large distances, damaged yet fundamentally able to rejuvenate. Boar can even carry acorns intact within their guts, excreting them complete with fertiliser. It has been found that for Iberian pears, whose seeds are destroyed by rodents, rabbits and deer, boar were invaluable in dispersing the seeds as viable propagules – intact.[2] Boar play a little-seen role in the propagation of the next generation of fruit trees – and as they increase once again in our countryside, so their role in planting the next generation of apples and pears will only become more apparent. It's past ten o'clock as we sneak away, leaving the boar to their moonlit feast.

In the past year, wild boar have crossed into Herefordshire – and their snouts are now getting to work disrupting the soils of the Malvern escarpment. It will be only a few years, we hope, before pork meets apple once more in this orchard. As so often, the advance of these hugely intelligent animals has been greatly underestimated. One local ecologist told Nancy and David that boar would never cross the M50 motorway, which separates the woodlands of the Forest of Dean from the Malverns. We can only presume that the boar looked both ways before crossing.

The tradition of disruptive pigs in orchards is nothing new. The charismatic Gloucester Old Spot, with its fleshy bat-like ears and peevish expression, was once known as the Orchard Pig. In nineteenth-century Herefordshire, pigs were often called upon to hoover rotten apples, long after the harvest had been brought in. Like our red admirals, they were renowned for their excesses, and could sometimes be found passed out after a heavy day's consumption; being brought around by a large trough of water to the snout. But the arrival of wilder orchard diggers, we feel, would transform this fruit-growing landscape. The free-roaming digging of boar would invigorate the richness of its soil; increasing small pools for newts and creating freshly tilled gardens in which new plants could take root. And far from disrupting the cider-making process, boar would sow new apples across this orchard landscape as they forage in the dark. But for many of our orchards to survive in the short term, there is only one gardener that can save them – and that is us.

Blue sky. White orchard. A long, deep freeze has simplified the landscape once more. The snow lies deep; the orchard's shapes loom as bold, crinkled figures. Black ivy berries are out in time for the Christmas wreath. Their pith alone packs as many calories as a Mars Bar.[3] A flash of orange denotes a redwing, then two, then three, diving down from the oaks to snatch the sour fruits before the blackbirds chase them off. But the ivy is far from under siege. By passing through the gut of these berry-thieves, the chemical composition of the ivy seed is changed. Certain toxins, likely to render it redundant in the soil, are removed. Now, with over one thousand starlings, blackbirds and winter thrushes moving in chattering scrums through the orchard, the ivy's next generation is assured.

Berry bushes are reliant on birds as their most important dispersers. In this regard, mistletoe has a long-developed ecosystem role. A study of mistletoe growing on junipers, now a rare tree on the denuded hills of much of upland Britain, found that more juniper berries sprout in stands where mistletoe is present. The mistletoe draws in an array of avian gluttons – and as they leave, so they also take with them, and sow, the seeds of the juniper as well.

There is no doubting, come winter, the extraordinary magnet that mistletoe berries provide. One December, I was watching ravens sky-dance over Maze Orchard when an unfamiliar, silver purring filled the air. Some triangular, plump, starling-sized birds glided around my head, around twenty in all, and piled into a single clump of mistletoe. Angry-faced, with black eye masks, punk crests and yellow and red sealing wax ornately stamped onto their wings, the waxwing invasion had finally reached Herefordshire. Widely heralded across our towns and cities, favouring supermarket car parks, pub gardens and industrial estates, waxwings arrive in numbers in Britain around one in every eight years. Here, they forsake the wild pine and birch forests of Scandinavia, where they nest in dense clumps of witch's hair lichen, for the berry-filled suburbs of our towns. Feeding on cotoneaster and rowan, both seren-dipitously in vogue among urban designers, it is remarkable how rarely waxwings are reported from the countryside. Or perhaps, it is remarkable how seldom they find the need to visit it, with rowans now such a rare sight in a landscape ever more devoid of wild berry trees. These waxwings, however, had done what waxwings are evolved to do and tracked down the largest berry hoard for miles around. Mistletoe, it seems, is one of their Christmas favourites.

Waxwings, to my mind, resemble Japanese paintings, with their soft salmon-greys and vivid sealing-waxed wings. At the same time, the painted white eye-mask, curling up under their eye, makes them appear perpetually suspicious. I sit for two hours watching them gorge, until, as is often the case, they appear almost unable to move. One bird sags distinctly to the left, as it comes to terms with quite how many berries it has eaten. Finally, trilling softly, the vora-cious horde chug away across the orchard, heading back towards the lights of a distant town. The urban jungle is calling them once more, but the berry bounty of the orchard has bought them another day's survival in their never-ending quest for food.

Mistletoe is in all respects a smart player in the orchard. As the winter goes on, we see it assert itself with ever more dominance. In recent decades, it has become ever more rampant in the orchard's warmer, milder winters. One of the reasons for this may come down to the fact that the Christmas mistletoe now has some new recruits. Until recently, only one all-year resident bird, the mistle thrush, was found to eat mistletoe berries on a regular basis. Winter thrushes play an important role in its spread too, the hordes of redwings and fieldfares wiping the sticky residue off their bills and so aiding the spread of the mistletoe onto new areas of the tree's surface. But the orchard's mistletoes now have an unobtrusive friend to aid them in their spread.

Until the past decade or so, blackcaps would migrate south to the Mediterranean in order to escape the harshness of the British frosts – but increasingly, no more. As many as ten blackcaps regularly winter here – and you will often find them moving quietly amid the mistletoe clumps. No longer migrating southwards, blackcaps find that the orchard provides them with a year-round bounty of fruits. In moving through the mistletoe, the blackcap chews away at single berries. It does not swallow them whole, and leaves the seeds. The seeds, however, are glutinous, sticking to the blackcap's bill. And in wiping its bill directly onto the branch, the blackcap spreads the orchard's mistletoe with toothpick-fine precision.

Yet while the blackcap may help, the true reason behind

the mistletoe's spread comes back to the orchard's ever-warming climate. As the winters are warmer than they were, so the orchard's apples endure fewer 'chill hours'. The sap more active in their veins, the mistletoe is more able to exploit the warmer, wetter conditions of winter; sucking nutrients, and water, from the tree. Come the following summer, and longer, drier periods, it continues this role, slowly desiccating the lifeblood of the apple. The tree will die first. The mistletoe, exhausting its own fuel, will follow.

Mistletoe, in itself, is not the culprit in these sad orchard deaths – our changing climate is. Orchard apple trees in particular, having evolved in the harsh continental winters of Kazakhstan as much as our own oceanic climate, require around a thousand hours, across a winter, when the temperature falls below 6 degrees Celsius – but above freezing. Without these dormant, refrigerated periods of sleep, the apples will face grave consequences the following season. In the atypically mild winter of 2015 to 2016, the orchard's apples failed to fall for long into their near-freezing slumber. The following winter, fungal infections were rife; able to infect the wet, living sap within the trees. By contrast, in a cold winter, an apple evacuates the water from its cells. The sucrose antifreeze inside keeps its tissues intact, but also renders these tissues harder to break down and attack. Metabolic activity in the tree is hampered by the cold – and so, likewise, is the spread of disease. Warm winters change all this. If 'alert' when it should be asleep, the tree's sap resources fall victim to the clutches of mistletoe which, instead of dying back, proliferates. It is a striking example of climate change, played out within the apparently idyllic Christmas setting of this timeless English landscape.

Early snowfall is never welcome news for the orchard's ageing trees. This December, we see what Nancy and David call a 'blue snow'. Heavy and packed with water, it sits like a death blanket on the mistletoe canopy of the old Broxwood Foxwhelp. When we visit a week later, this beloved veteran has fallen. Remarkably, the entire trunk has split down the centre – as if some cosmic axe has been riven through its crown.

By the time veteran apples are killed in this way, their fate is often already sealed. The wet clay soils of this part of the Malverns are unforgiving. Only the strongest rootstocks of the old standards will stand the test of time. 'It's like a loose tooth,' says Nancy. 'As soon as the tree begins to work loose, sooner or later, it will be uprooted. The weight of the mistletoe and the snow give it the final push.' As the winter goes on, the death of the veterans becomes a familiar story. But at this time of tree death and the loss of old friends, David and Nancy are already preparing to plant the next generation, ensuring the survival of their prized ancient stock.

Come December, they both spring to life in felling clumps of mistletoe that could drain the tree of life or conspire with the snow to bring the older apples down. Mistletoe on younger trees is left, as is that growing in the lower clefts of well-established trees. While Nancy is equivocal about pruning, she and David will 'rebalance' those trees with twisted limbs, where one misshapen branch could jeopardise the balance, and future, of the whole. An old Herefordshire saying, passed down to Nancy, is that when rebalancing a standard, one should be able to throw a top hat through the middle of the tree. If your work has been successful, the hat will emerge on the other side. This adage, which I've yet to see tested in the orchard, comes down to the fact that too many intertwining and touching branches can be bad news come the winter gales, triggering a 'pick-up-sticks' effect that can increase the chances of the tree being brought down. Careful as always, David and Nancy leave the tree's most valuable natural assets. The dead snags beloved by woodpeckers, and the epicormic growths of the Strawberry Norman's carbuncles, will be left untouched. But in balancing the veteran apples in this way, several years may be added to their valuable lives.

Whereas many orchard growers relentlessly prune, David and Nancy take a gentler approach. Older trees can be shocked by radical pruning, and few of the trees – even the most productive – are strongly pruned. Nancy's approach to pruning, which she learned in turn from her father, has been very conservative, and while each year she and David balance the trees, and prevent too many of their branches from touching, the apples and pears retain a wild dignity, growing largely in peace, unshocked by the sudden severance of limbs in their old age. And the fruits just keep on falling.

When David and Nancy come to plant the next generation of apple trees, they face a recurring problem. Since the late 1960s, commercial orchard planting has prioritised short-term yields over the longevity and stability of once-mighty orchard standards. Smaller rootstocks were instead developed, so that trees could grow more like bushes. Not needing to live so long, these new varieties do not need to be robust enough to handle so much weight, especially in the crown of the tree. These modern, short-lived apple breeds do, certainly, yield fruit earlier – in greater profusion albeit lower quality. But in the unforgiving clay soils of this part of Herefordshire, these weaker breeds will die at just fifteen years old. This, of course, means that most modern orchard trees never attain the creviced grandeur, insect communities, nesting nooks or dead wood needed to make them of invaluable use to the creatures of the wildwood.

Nancy's old standard trees, however, still have many a thing to teach the growers of newer, commercial orchards. Many of these veterans, planted well before the 1940s, have attained strange shapes indeed – their lateral branches grow stocky and thick, and thus, even when crowded with clusters of apples, will bend rather than break. Yet knack-ered and battered as these storm-hardened veterans appear, the orchard in its entirety, old trees and new, still produces 100 tonnes of fruit in the course of a season.

In recent years, David has begun the process that will regenerate the orchard in the years to come. As zealously as a conservationist breeding wild cats or tigers for release into the wild, David has got to work grafting the next generation of his most special breeds, such as the Kingston and Barland, onto newly planted rootstock. Apple seeds do not produce the same fruit as the apple from whence they came, so this is where grafting comes in. Scions – budding branches taken from the target tree – are generally around one year in age. Cut in late autumn or winter with sharp shears, your ideal scion is around half a centimetre thick. It can then be kept over the winter.

Only next spring, as the orchard's trees begin to wake up once more, and the buds of the rootstock tree are ready to open, will David graft these precious scions. It is a surgical process, and done with great precision. The rootstock is cut at an upwards angle, and the scion at an acute downward angle; a long cut, around two centimetres in length. As the bottom, dead part of the scion is cut off, the fresh, green cells – dormant below – are revealed. Into both the rootstock and the scion are cut 'tongues'. This allows the cambium cells in the wood – those actively dividing cells that fuel the growth of new plant matter – to fuse together. Once these tongues are cut, then, like a fine dovetail joint, the rootstock and the scion lock, flush – the one forever bound to the other. Floral tape is wrapped around the point where scion meets root – and slowly, under pressure from the carefully administered bandage, the two will fuse. Cells fuse into cells – and five hundred years of orchard cultivation finds new roots in the ground of the orchard, as the year draws to its end.

DECEMBER

It's late afternoon on New Year's Eve. An eerie hush blankets the orchard. The snow has locked the apples away. Sad and mute, once-warring thrushes cluster in the hedgerows as the fading light turns them to grumpy, huddled shapes. The old apples lean, it seems, a little more than at the month's beginning; their outstretched forms pleading in silence. Below the furrowed tentacles of pears, a tidy rank of new trees lies carefully planted. These tiny pioneers stand bolt upright: young cadets, frozen in a never-ending salute to their elders. The deep blue dims and the old trees fade. As the moon silvers the orchard's wrinkled skin, only fierce orchard robins will sing for this vanishing world.

ACKNOWLEDGEMENTS

We are indebted to many people in writing this book, but none more than Nancy and David, who have allowed us to make England's finest orchard our playground for now more than eight years, and without whose inspirational efforts to farm and conserve the land against all odds, this book would never have been possible to write.

In addition, special thanks must go to orchard specialists Keith Turner and Jim Chapman, for their help in advising upon the rich culture and history of orchards, and naturalist and producer Steve Nicholls for his assistance.

We would like to thank the Herefordshire Orchard Groups, Herefordshire Wildlife Trust's Orchard Origins project, the Gloucestershire Orchard Trust, the Wyre Forest Study Group, the People's Trust for Endangered Species, and all other traditional orchard groups for their ongoing support and love of these rich habitats, and the amazing science and orchard recovery that has come of their work.

Especial thanks go to our dedicated publisher Myles Archibald, our excellent editors Hazel Eriksson and Sally Partington, and our devoted artists Sophie Tallis and Tom Cabot. In addition, we would like to thank our families and our partners, Louise and Helena, for their unerring patience with two men who spend far more time than usual peering into rotting vaults of wood.

ENDNOTES

APPLES AND BEARS

1. Harris, Stephen A., Robinson, Julian P., Juniper, Barrie E. (2002), 'Genetic Clues to the Origin of the Apple', *Trends in Genetics*, volume 18, issue 8, pages 426–30. DOI:10.1016/S0168-9525(02)02689-6
2. BBC Future/Chris Baraniuk. 2016. Kazakhstan's treasure trove of wildly-flavoured apples. https://www.bbc.com/future/article/20160523-kazakhstans-treasure-trove-of-wildly-flavoured-apples
3. *The Guardian*/Alys Fowler. 2014. Gardens: why we need to protect Kazakhstan's apples. https://www.theguardian.com/lifeandstyle/2014/nov/08/kazakhstan-wild-apples-endangered-alys-fowler
4. McLellan, B. N., Hovey, F. W., (2001), 'Natal Dispersal of Grizzly Bears', *Canadian Journal of Zoology*, issue 79, pages 838–44. DOI: 10.1139/Z01-051
5. Macdonald, B., *Rebirding*. Pelagic Publishing Ltd., Exeter, 2019. Pages 4–19
6. Outram, A.K., et al (2009), 'The Earliest Horse Harnessing and Milking', *Science*, 06 Mar: 1332–1335
7. Luby, J., Forsline, P., Aldwinckle, H.S., Bus, V. and Geibel, M. (2001), 'Silk Road Apples—Collection, Evaluation, and Utilization of *Malus sieversii* from Central Asia', *HortScience*, issue 36, pages 225–31. DOI:10.21273/HORTSCI.36.2.225
8. Cornille, A., Gladieux, P., Smulders, M.J.M., Roldán-Ruiz, I., Laurens, F., Le Cam, B., et al (2012), 'New Insight into the History of Domesticated Apple: Secondary Contribution of the European Wild Apple to the Genome of Cultivated Varieties', *PLoS Genet*, volume 8, issue 5. e1002703. DOI:10.1371/journal.pgen.1002703
Duan, N., Bai, Y., Sun, H., et al (2017), 'Genome Re-sequencing Reveals the History of Apple and Supports a Two-stage Model for Fruit Enlargement', *Nat Commun*, volume 8, issue 249. DOI:10.1038/s41467-017-00336-7

ENDNOTES

9. Homer, *The Odyssey*. Translated by Barry B. Powell. *EBook Collection (EBSCOhost)*. Oxford University Press, Oxford, 2014

10. The Judgement of Paris is a Greek myth with no one, defined source. On this occasion it was read about from: Ovid, *Heroides*. Penguin Classics, reprinted 1990. This is not the first source of the myth.

11. Pseudo-Apollodorus, *Bibliotheca*, 3. 9. 2

12. Pliny the Elder, *Natural History: A Selection*. Penguin Classics, reprinted 1991

13. Collins Dictionaries, *Collins English Dictionary Complete and Unabridged*. Collins, London, 2018

14. Mills, D., *A Dictionary of British Place Names*. Oxford University Press, Oxford, revised edition 2011

15. Gautier, A. (2013), 'Cooking and Cuisine in Late Anglo-Saxon England', *Anglo-Saxon England*, issue 41, pages 373–406. https://www.jstor.org/stable/26326779

16. Appleton with Eaton/Trevor Rowley. A brief history of Appleton with Eaton. https://www.appleton-eaton.org/history

17. Morgan, J., *The Book of Pears: The Definitive History and Guide to Over 500 Varieties*. Ebury Press, London, 2015

18. *The Guardian*/Karen Homer. 2011. Save England's real apples. https://www.theguardian.com/commentisfree/2011/mar/14/apple-britain-gala-traditional

19. Braekman, W.L. (1985), 'Bollard's Middle English Book of Planting and Grafting and its Background', *Studia Neophilologica*, volume 57, issue 1, pages 19–39. DOI: 10.1080/00393278508587901

20. Jim Chapman (Gloucestershire orchard historian) per comms to Ben Macdonald, Oct 2019

21. Jarvis, B., 'Cider, Perry, Fruit Wines and Other Alcoholic Fruit Beverages'. In Arthey, D. and Ashurst, P.R. (eds), *Fruit Processing*. Springer, Boston, 1996

22. Jim Chapman (Gloucestershire orchard historian) per comms to Ben Macdonald, Oct 2019

23. Chapman, L., *Anne Boleyn in London*. Pen & Sword Books Ltd., London, 2016

24. Lambarde, W., *A Perambulation of Kent Conteining the Description, Hystorie, and Customes of that Shire*. Baldwin, Chadock and Joy, London, 1576

25. Saunders, R., *The Apple Book*. Frances Lincoln, revised edition, 2010

26. Lambarde, W., *A Perambulation of Kent Conteining the Description, Hystorie, and Customes of that Shire*. Baldwin, Chadock and Joy, London, 1576

27. Lovegrove, R., *Silent Fields: The Long Decline of a Nation's Wildlife*. Oxford University Press, Oxford, 2008

28. Watson, B., *Cider, Hard and Sweet: History, Traditions, and Making Your Own*. W. W. Norton & Company, 2013
29. Felton, S., *On the Portraits of English Authors on Gardening*. Palala Press, 2015
30. Witheridge Historical Archive. Apples and cider. http://www.witheridge-historical-archive.com/apples.htm
31. Alexander, K.N.A., 'The Links Between Forest History and Biodiversity: The Invertebrate Fauna of Ancient Pasture-woodlands in Britain and its Conservation'. In Kirby, K.J. and Watkins, C. (eds), *The Ecological History of European Forests*. CAB International, Wallingford
    Alexander has argued widely for a broken wood-pasture landscape based on beetle evidence. See also:
    Alexander, K., et al (2006), 'The Value of Different Tree and Shrub Species to Wildlife', *British Wildlife*, issue 18, pages 18–28
    Alexander, K.N.A. (2014), 'Non-intervention Versus Intervention – But Balanced? I Think Not', *British Ecological Society Bulletin*, issue 45, pages 36–7
32. Fortune, D., *Glastonbury: Avalon of the Heart*. Red Wheel Weiser, 2003
33. Watson, B., *Cider, Hard and Sweet: History, Traditions, and Making Your Own*. W. W. Norton & Company, 2013
34. Bull, H.G. and Hogg, R., *The Herefordshire Pomona*. Jakeman and Carver, 1876
35. Badby History. Catalogue of plants found in the Badby area around 1840. http://www.badbyhistory.org.uk/nature.html#_plantlist
36. White, G., *The Natural History of Selborne*. Penguin Classics, reprinted 1977
37. Balston, R.J., *Notes on the Birds of Kent*. General Books LLC., 2010
38. As above
39. *The Independent*/Peter Popham. 1995. Squeezed till the pippins squeak. https://www.independent.co.uk/life-style/squeezed-till-the-pippins-squeak-1616636.html
40. People's Trust for Endangered Species. Traditional orchard decline. https://ptes.org/campaigns/traditional-orchard-project/traditional-orchard-decline/
    Using a fantastic tool from the People's Trust for Endangered Species, you can now find your local community orchard online here: https://ptes.org/campaigns/traditional-orchard-project/orchard-network/community-orchards/
41. Smart, M.J. and Winnall, R.A. (eds) (2006), 'The Biodiversity of Three Traditional Orchards Within the Wyre Forest SSSI in Worcestershire: A Survey by the Wyre Forest Study Group', English Nature Report No. 707

ENDNOTES

JANUARY

1. British Trust for Ornithology. Fieldfare. https://www.bto.org/our-science/projects/gbw/gardens-wildlife/garden-birds/a-z-garden-birds/fieldfare
2. Goodwin, D., *British Thrushes*. Collins, London, 1978
3. Peterken, G.F., et al (1992), 'Old-growth Conservation Within British Upland Forestry Plantations', *Forestry*, volume 65, issue 2, pages 127–44

FEBRUARY

1. Yoon, S.H. and Park, S. (2011), 'A Mechanical Analysis of Woodpecker Drumming and its Application to Shock-absorbing Systems', *Bioinspiration & Biomechanics*, volume 6, issue 1. DOI:10.1088/1748-3182/6/1/016003
2. National Perry Pear Centre. Betty Prosser. https://www.nationalperrypearcentre.org.uk/pear/betty-prosser/
3. Martell, C., *Native Apples of Gloucestershire*. Gloucestershire Orchard Trust, 2014
4. Orchard owners (requesting anonymity) per comms to Ben Macdonald, October 2019
5. Orchard owners (requesting anonymity) per comms to Ben Macdonald, October 2019
6. British Birds. 2016. Eurasian jay's mimicry of tawny owl to deter carrion crow. https://britishbirds.co.uk/article/eurasian-jays-mimicry-tawny-owl-deter-carrion-crow/
7. Hindmarsh, A.M. (1984), 'Vocal Mimicry in Starlings', *Behaviour*, volume 90, issue 4, pages 302–24
8. Balmer, D., Gillings, S., Caffrey, B., et al., *Bird Atlas 2007–11: The Breeding and Wintering Birds of Britain and Ireland*. BTO, Thetford, 2013 Future references to bird population increase and decline will, unless specified, be taken from this definitive source of information on the recent fortunes of British birds.

MARCH

1. *The Guardian*. Mark Smith and agencies. 2015. Weasel-riding-woodpecker picture prompts weighty Twitter debate. https://www.theguardian.com/environment/2015/mar/03/weasel-and-woodpecker-combo-soar-to-top-of-online-charts
2. Balmer, D., Gillings, S., Caffrey, B., et al., *Bird Atlas 2007–11: The Breeding and Wintering Birds of Britain and Ireland*. BTO, Thetford, 2013

3. Newton, I., *The Sparrowhawk*. Poyser Monographs, Bloomsbury, London, 2010
4. British Trust for Ornithology. Goshawk. https://www.bto.org/understanding-birds/species-focus/goshawk
5. British Trust for Ornithology. 2011. Coal tit. https://www.bto.org/sites/default/files/shared_documents/gbw/associated_files/bird-table-65-coal-tit-species-focus.pdf
6. Hansell, M.H., *Built by Animals: The Natural History of Animal Architecture*. Oxford University Press, 2007
7. Three papers document the fascinating aspects of long-tailed tit behaviour outlined in this chapter:
McGowan, A., Hatchwell, B.J., Woodburn, R.J.W. (2003), 'The Effect of Helping Behaviour on the Survival of Juvenile and Adult Long-tailed Tits *Aegithalos caudatus*', *Journal of Animal Ecology*, volume 72, issue 3, pages 491–9. DOI:10.1046/j.1365-2656.2003.00719.x
Hatchwell, J., Ross, D.J., Fowlie, M.K., McGowan, A. (2001), 'Kin Discrimination in Cooperatively Breeding Long-tailed Tits', *Proceedings of the Royal Society of London: Biological Sciences*, volume 26, issue 1470, pages 885–90. DOI:10.1098/rspb.2001.1598. PMC 1088684
Sharp, S.P., Simeoni, M., Hatchwell, B. (2008), 'Dispersal of Sibling Coalitions Promotes Helping Among Immigrants in a Cooperatively Breeding Bird', *Proceedings of the Royal Society of London: Biological Sciences*, volume 275, issue 1647, pages 2125–30. DOI:10.1098/rspb.2008.0398. PMC 2603207

APRIL

1. Kay, Q.O.N. (1985), 'Nectar From Willow Catkins as a Food Source for Blue Tits, *Bird Study*, volume 32, issue 1, pages 40–4. DOI: 10.1080/00063658509476853
2. Smith, N.D. (1990), The Ecology of the Slow-worm (*Anguis Fragilis L.*) in Southern England. University of Southampton, Doctoral Thesis, 229 pages. PURE UUID: 70e920dd-34a7-4ac2-861c-a74b839744c3
3. Broughton, et al (2011), 'Nest-sites, Breeding Failure and Causes of Non-breeding in a Population of British Marsh Tits *Poecile palustris*', *Bird Study*, volume 58
4. Barton, K., 'Verfluchte Kreaturen: Lichtenbergs "Proben seltsamen Aberglaubens" und die Logik der Hexen- und Insektenverfolgung im "Malleus Maleficarum"'. In Joost, U., Neumann, A. (eds), *Lichtenberg-Jahrbuch*. Saarbrücken (SDV Saarländische Druckerei und Verlag), 2004. In German
5. Marren, P., Mabey, R., *Bugs Britannica*. Chatto & Windus, London 2010

ENDNOTES

MAY

1. Scott Aker is Supervisory Research Horticulturist at the Gardens Unit of the Agricultural Research Service: scott.aker@usda.gov
2. The complex science of how trees go to sleep and wake up is here enormously condensed for reasons of brevity. The very best readily accessible yet utterly comprehensive title detailing the internal lives of trees is arguably:
Wohlleben, P., *The Hidden Life of Trees*, William Collins, London, 2017.
3. Holloway, S., *The Historical Atlas of Breeding Birds in Britain and Ireland 1875–1900*. Poyser, London, 1996
4. Cambridgeshire bird ringing. Studying flycatchers. http://cambridgeshirebirdringing.org/spofl-current/

JUNE

1. This statistic is widely sourced and occasionally challenged or misquoted but originates from: Chauvin, R. (1956), 'Les Facteurs qui Gouvernent la Ponte Chez la Reine des Abeilles', *Insect Sociaux*, volume 3, pages 499–504
For more information on honeybee social structure, see also the excellent: Winston, M.L., *The Biology of the Honey Bee*. Harvard University Press, Boston, 1991
2. Quicke, D.L.J. and Fitton, M.G. (1995), 'Ovipositor Steering Mechanisms in Parasitic Wasps of the Families Gasteruptiidae and Aulacidae (Hymenoptera)', *Proceedings of the Royal Society of London: Biological Sciences*, volume 261, issue 1360. DOI:10.1098/rspb.1995.0122
3. As above
4. Macdonald, B., *Rebirding*. Pelagic Publishing Ltd., Exeter, 2019
5. Lewis, A.J.G., et al (2009), 'The Decline of the Willow Tit in Britain', *British Birds*, volume 102, pages 386–93

JULY

1. Sanchez-Bayo, F. and Wyckhuys, K.A.G. (2019), 'Worldwide Decline of the Entomofauna: A Review of its Drivers', *Biological Conservation*, volume 232, pages 8–27

AUGUST

1. Schwintzer, C.R. and Tjepkema, J.D. (eds), *The Biology of Frankia and Actinorhizal Plants*. Academic Press, Inc., New York, 1990

2. Zatonski, J. (2016), 'Population of Common Swift in Poznań (Poland) and Ecosystem Services Provided by it', *Ekonomia i Środowiski*, volume 4, pages 263–73

3. In recent years, series such as the BBC's *Planet Earth* have popularised the idea of the zombie fungus – and the chilling prospect of mind control. The now infamous *Cordyceps* fungus of tropical South America featured again in Netflix's *Our Planet* series. *Cordyceps* is a fungus that infects not only the bodies but the *minds* of its hosts. Once parasitised, its commonest prey, ants, begin to exhibit strange and irrational behaviour. Eventually, and entirely against its own voluntary instincts, the ant crawls up a stem, and locks its jaws down hard – all at the mental behest of the fungus, which now controls all of the ant's motor functions. Then, a long, thin spore erupts from the ant's head – scattering the fungus onto the next generation of hapless ants. It is a natural history sequence that once seen, is never forgotten. By performing this macabre act, the *Cordyceps* fungus spreads itself far and wide throughout the rainforest. At the same time, while seemingly sadistic, it regulates the abundance of any one species, by keeping populations of defoliating species, like the leafcutter ants, in check.

4. Watson, D.W., et al (1993), 'Behavioral Fever Response of *Musca domestica* (Diptera: Muscidae) to Infection by *Entomophthora muscae* (Zygomycetes: Entomophthorales)', *Journal of Invertebrate Pathology*, volume 61, issue 1, pages 10–16
    Note that the species infecting hoverflies in the orchard is *Entomophthora syrphii*, a closely-related pathogen.

5. Keightley T., *The Fairy Mythology*. Nabu Press, 2010

6. *The Guardian*/Philip Hoare. 2018. Britain is plagued by wasps – here are five reasons to celebrate. https://www.theguardian.com/environ-ment/shortcuts/2018/aug/12/
    wasps-plague-britain-five-reasons-to-celebrate

SEPTEMBER

1. Soil Association. The impact of glyphosate on soil health. 5.4 Million acres is 23 per cent of the 23.07 million acres of farmed land in the UK. https://www.soilassociation.org/media/7202/glyphosate-and-soil-health-full-report.pdf

2. Soil Association. The impact of glyphosate on soil health. https://www.soilassociation.org/media/7202/glyphosate-and-soil-health-full-report.pdf

3. Lipkin A., et al (2002), 'Novel Insecticidal Toxins from the Venom of the Spider *Segestria florentina*', *Toxicon*, volume 40, issue 2, pages 125–30

ENDNOTES

4. A case of arachnidism by *Segestria Florentina* (Rossi, 1790) (Araneae Segestriidae) in Salento. http://siba-ese.unisalento.it/index.php/thalassiasal/article/viewFile/2286/1932
As it is evident from the different cases illustrated elsewhere, the bite of *S. florentina* is not dangerous for humans.
5. Eurobats/Peter Lina. 2017. Common names of European bats. https://www.eurobats.org/sites/default/files/documents/publications/publication_series/EUROBATS_PublSeries_No7_2nd_edition_2017.pdf
6. Bat Conservation Trust. 2019. Bats in Scotland. https://cdn.bats.org.uk/pdf/Scottish-bats-2019.pdf?mtime=20190412121246
7. Lewanzik, D. and Goerlitz, H. (2018), 'Continued Source Level Reduction During Attack in the Low-amplitude Bat *Barbastella barbastellus* Prevents Moth Evasive Flight', *Functional Ecology*. DOI:10.1111/1365-2435.13073
8. Bat Conservation Trust. 2010. Noctule bat. https://cdn.bats.org.uk/pdf/About%20Bats/noctule_11.02.13.pdf?mtime=20181101151302

OCTOBER

1. *The Guardian*/Emma Sheppard. 2017. After Brexit people will fall in love with English apples again. https://www.theguardian.com/small-business-network/2017/apr/28/after-brexit-english-apples-bramley-starkey
2. *The Guardian*/Paul Evans. 2018. Country diary: the hedgerows are transformed, as if by magic. https://www.theguardian.com/environment/2018/sep/12/country-diary-the-hedgerows-are-transformed-as-if-by-magic
3. Lovegrove, R., *Silent Fields: The Long Decline of a Nation's Wildlife*. Oxford University Press, Inc. (OUP USA), New York, 2008

NOVEMBER

1. *The Guardian*/Paul Brown. 2019. Specieswatch: the English oak and its chattering friend. https://www.theguardian.com/environment/2019/sep/24/specieswatch-the-english-oak-and-its-chattering-friend.
Also: Bossema. 1979. Jays and oaks: an eco-ethological study of a symbiosis. https://www.jstor.org/stable/4533982?seq=1
2. Dobrowolska, D. and Wiatrowska, B. (2019), 'Dispersal Distance and Burial Mode of Acorns in Eurasian days *Garrulus glandarius* in European Temperate Forests', *Acta Ornithologica*, volume 53, issue 2, pages 155–62. DOI: 10.3161/00016454A02018. 53.2.005
3. The fascinating world of the robin's nocturnal singing, and the song division between males and females, is widely available in literature and

online, but the following peer-reviewed papers cover this in detail:
Kriner, E. and Schwabl, H. (1991), 'Control of Winter Song and
Territorial Aggression of Female Robins (*Erithacus rubecula*) by
Testosterone', *Ethology*, volume 87, pages 37–44.
DOI:10.1111/j.1439-0310.1991.tb01186.x
Schwabl, H. (1992), 'Winter and Breeding Territorial Behaviour and
Levels of Reproductive Hormones of Migratory European
Robins', *Ornis Scandinavica (Scandinavian Journal of Ornithology)*,
volume 23, issue 3, pages 271–76. DOI:10.2307/3676649
East, M. (1982), 'Time-Budgeting by European Robins *Erithacus
rubecula*: Inter and Intrasexual Comparisons during Autumn, Winter and
Early Spring', *Ornis Scandinavica (Scandinavian Journal of Ornithology)*,
volume 13, issue 2, pages 85–93. DOI:10.2307/3676194
Hoelzel, A.R. (1986), 'Song Characteristics and Response to Playback of
Male and Female Robins *Erithacus rubecula*', *Ibis*, volume 128, pages
115–27. DOI:10.1111/j.1474-919X.1986.tb02098.x
Fuller, R., Warren, P. and Gaston, K. (2007), 'Daytime Noise Predicts
Nocturnal Singing in Urban Robins', *Biology Letters*, volume 3, pages
368–70. DOI:10.1098/rsbl.2007.0134
4. The amazing finds centre around the orchards of Colwall village.
    Without giving away the exact location of our orchard, which we have
    agreed with its owners not to do, we can say that this is the same
    orchard ecosystem, and that these findings are highly relevant to our
    orchard – and to the Malvern's traditional orchards in general. The same
    will go for the richest orchards across Herefordshire and Worcestershire.
    Dr Keith Alexander. 2009. Colwall Orchards invertebrate study. https://
    ptes.org/wp-content/uploads/2016/07/Colwall-Orchards-Invertebrate-
    Survey-2009.pdf

DECEMBER

1. Volker Sommer et al. Not eating like a pig: European wild boar wash
    their food. https://discovery.ucl.ac.uk/id/eprint/1539371/1/Sommer_
    Anim_Cog_Pig_Food_Wash_Sommer_et_al_Subm.pdf
2. Fedriani, J. (2009), 'Seed Dispersal in the Iberian Pear, *Pyrus
    bourgaeana*: A Role for Infrequent Mutualists', *Ecoscience*, volume 16,
    pages 311–21. DOI:10.2980/16-3-3253
3. RSPB. Birds and berries. https://www.rspb.org.uk/birds-and-wildlife/
    natures-home-magazine/birds-and-wildlife-articles/features/birds-and-
    berries/

INDEX

INDEX

INDEX

INDEX